The Henge
Monuments

NEW ASPECTS OF ANTIQUITY

General Editor: COLIN RENFREW

Consulting Editor for the Americas: JEREMY A. SABLOFF

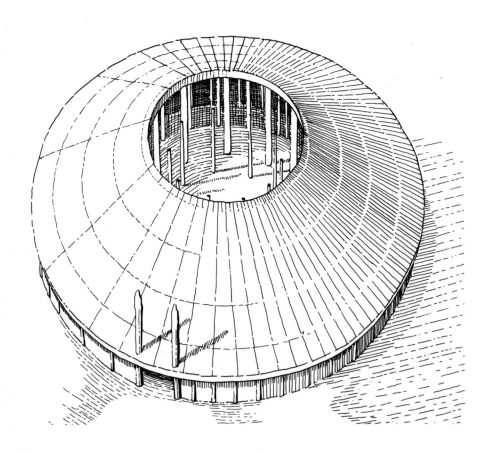

GEOFFREY WAINWRIGHT

The Henge Monuments

Ceremony and Society in Prehistoric Britain

with 111 illustrations, 8 in color

 THAMES AND HUDSON

Title page: A detail of fig. 30, the Southern Circle at Durrington Walls.

© 1989 Thames and Hudson Ltd, London

First published in the USA in 1990 by Thames and Hudson Inc.,
500 Fifth Avenue, New York, New York 10110

Library of Congress Catalog Card Number 89-50632

Typeset in Monophoto Sabon

Printed and bound in Yugoslavia

CONTENTS

GENERAL EDITOR'S FOREWORD

This book is devoted to one of the most remarkable episodes of British archaeology. It is one which we may, without immodesty, claim as among the most interesting and intriguing in world prehistory. For it describes the emergence of a society in the early farming period in Britain which, at about the same time that the pyramids of Egypt were being built, could produce such extraordinary and original monuments as Stonehenge, as the great stone circles at Avebury, as that colossal earthen mound Silbury Hill, and as those remote and arresting circles of stone far to the north in Orkney, the Stones of Stenness and the Ring of Brodgar.

This work by Geoffrey Wainwright represents, moreover, the culmination of a process of research which we can trace back for more than 60 years, to the early days of aerial photography, and the realization that the great stone monuments such as Stonehenge and Avebury formed part of a very much wider pattern. The investigation of that pattern, not least by Dr Wainwright's own excavations at three of the most important ceremonial sites, has been one of the most satisfying stories in the archaeology of recent decades. It now allows us to see all these monuments as part of a larger picture: it is one where we now understand the chronology, we are well informed about the economy and can even claim an increasingly clear picture of the society.

This is particularly satisfying, since for centuries the nature and origin of these great monuments had been the subject of speculation. In the early seventeenth century the great Renaissance architect Inigo Jones visited Stonehenge at the invitation of King James I and offered a conjectural reconstruction. In the eighteenth century the imaginative, indeed romantic, William Stukeley made detailed plans of Stonehenge and Avebury – they are still valued by archaeologists and found useful today – and attributed both sites to the activities of the mysterious Druids. In the early nineteenth century Sir Richard Colt Hoare, who had himself pioneered a series of excavations of the prehistoric monuments of southern England, could confess complete uncertainty as to their date or their significance. Writing of the impressive stone tomb of New

Grange in Ireland, in a passage which admirably expresses the doubts and confusions of the time he could say:

I fear both its authors and its original destination will ever remain unknown. Conjecture may wonder over its wild and spacious domains but will never bring home with it either truth or conviction. Alike will the histories of those stupendous temples at AVEBURY and STONEHENGE which grace my native country remain involved in obscurity and oblivion.

This fog of confusion has been banished within our own time. As Dr Wainwright so clearly describes, the first significant step was taken by an aviator in 1925, Squadron Leader Insall. One of the pioneers of aerial photography, he recorded a prehistoric enclosure with a circle of pits or post-holes, the remnants of a circle of wooden uprights, which was soon dubbed 'Woodhenge' out of respect for its more famous neighbour, Stonehenge. The site was excavated over the three following years, and was followed by the excavation of an analogous monument near Avebury. It was in 1932 that Thomas Kendrick and Christopher Hawkes coined the new term 'henge' or 'henge monument' to designate this class of circular enclosure of the early farming period (the British later Neolithic) of which more and more examples were being recognized, mainly through aerial photography.

As Dr Wainwright describes, it became clear that among them were a few of very much greater scale, of which Avebury itself was the most famous. The other three major sites in southern England – Durrington Walls, Marden and Mount Pleasant – are now household words among archaeologists. Each of them was excavated by Dr Wainwright in a series of brilliant excavation seasons between 1966 and 1971. Among the most important findings, which he sets out here, was the discovery that such sites frequently contained massive circular timber structures, comparable in form but larger in scale than that first timber circle excavated at Woodhenge 40 years earlier.

Through Geoffrey Wainwright's work, and that of other archaeologists in this country, a pattern has now emerged. It is a pattern which has gained greatly in coherence by the application of radiocarbon analysis, so that it is now possible to date these sites. As Dr Wainwright indicates, we can now recognize an earlier phase of monument building. This is followed by something of a recession, lasting as much as 500 years, and is then succeeded by a new phase of increased activity, during which the great henge monuments, as well as that smaller but more famous stone circle at Stonehenge itself, were built.

As the excavator of these three great henge sites, Dr Wainwright writes with unique authority. He is admirably placed to review the enormous increases in our knowledge of Neolithic Britain which have come about in recent years. It is a story which merits attention at a world level. For this is one of those encouraging cases where, by the techniques of archaeology alone (in collaboration, of course, with the environmental sciences) it has been possible to reconstruct a remarkably complex prehistoric society with an elaborate ceremonial life, and to rescue it from what had earlier seemed an inevitable 'obscurity and oblivion'.

Colin Renfrew

INTRODUCTION

By 2000 BC much of Europe had already been divided fairly rigidly into territories by societies which possessed defined geographical frontiers, some evidence for class distinctions and with surprisingly little evidence for long distance trade. There are a number of pointers to large and prosperous populations at this time in parts of Europe. In the south-east, large settlements occur associated with several hundred graves in a single cemetery. In Malta at the Hal Saflieni rock-cut tombs, some 7,000 people are estimated to have been buried during the third millennium BC. In north-west Europe and Britain huge earthworks and monuments in timber and stone are evidence for a large and organized workforce working to plans defined and implemented by a central authority.

The period encompassed by this book occurs at the end of the nearly 2,000 years which intervened in Britain between the first emergence of Neolithic farming communities in about 3500 BC and the development of a technology based on the working of bronze in about 1700 BC. The majority of the recorded sites of the period in southern England are those represented by banks and ditches, or occasionally by large stones, which are now in many cases worn away after millennia of ploughing. The structures and buildings that were of timber have not survived as visible remains, leaving a substantial gap in our knowledge and consequent assessment of that era. Stonehenge illustrates this point. In the latter part of the twentieth century, it has achieved its renown because 4,000 years ago it was built of stone and not of wood or earth. Originally it was surrounded by a ditch 2 m deep and a bank 2 m high – both now flattened into an insignificant hump. In the 30 square kilometres of the environs of Stonehenge are more than 400 burial mounds of the second millennium BC alone. Some survive, but most have been damaged by repeated ploughing, or levelled completely so that nothing shows on the ground. About 3 km north-east of Stonehenge is Durrington Walls, a circular enclosure on a far grander scale, but the earthworks have been levelled by ploughing and because the internal structures were of timber, they have long since decayed to leave no trace on the turf where the posts had once stood. Stonehenge is the only stone-built monument in a landscape once containing hundreds of earth and wood structures and its isolation today belies the former importance of its environs. On the whole, these eroded remains, which represent millennia of settlement, are clustered on the chalklands – the Marlborough Downs, Salisbury Plain, Cranborne Chase and the Dorset Downs. They are represented by burial mounds, both long and round, some circular earthwork enclosures of different types, and some sparse evidence for industrial activity represented by flint mines. Very few domestic sites are known and these are indicated by clusters of shallow pits, whose ultimate use was for the disposal of rubbish, or simply by scatters of stone tools on the surface of ploughed fields. Similarly, the artifacts found are not visually impressive and consist of fragmentary pots, bone and flint cutting and scraping implements and some polished axes of flint and stone. The exotic objects of copper, bronze and occasionally gold, which began to appear in the area towards the end of the period with which we are concerned, were few in number and must have been restricted to a minority amongst a population who were still using stone for their implements.

Two of the principal characteristics of the larger ceremonial monuments in Neolithic and Bronze Age Wessex which are the subject of this book, are size and 'monumentality' combined with longevity. Monuments such as Avebury, Silbury Hill, Stonehenge, the Dorset Cursus and Durrington Walls have no rivals for sheer scale elsewhere in the country. The monuments were not only great feats of engineering construction but must also have entailed a considerable commitment of human and material resources. There is some morphological similarity between them but it would be unwise to assume from this that they necessarily played similar rôles within ancient societies. This book attempts not only to describe the monuments and the programme of work which led to their recognition, but also to explain the rôle of these monuments in the societies of the time and the ways in which they may have facilitated the workings of those societies. The territory within which these events took place is prehistoric Wessex – those counties of mid-southern England where Stonehenge, Avebury and many lesser monuments are found. The period is those formative 2,000 years between the first appearance of farming communities and the development of metallurgy in 1700 BC, and first we must examine the nature of the evidence with which we have to deal.

CHAPTER ONE

THE NATURE
OF THE EVIDENCE

Around 2000 BC there became established in Britain a tradition of constructing ceremonial circles of earth, stone and timber. It was an essentially British phenomenon, typified in the public mind with Stonehenge and chanting Druids against a background of sarsen trilithons, the peace convoy, blue uniforms and a fantasia of books on prehistoric astronomy and ley-lines. Stonehenge is perhaps fortunately unique in possessing a lintelled structure, but over 900 other stone circles are known in Britain and Ireland where they are widely distributed all over the highland and upland areas from the outer Hebrides and the Orkneys to south-west Ireland and Somerset and Dorset. There are many superstitions concerning the bad luck attendant on any person moving or damaging the stones of the circles, and it is probable that some have survived because of country traditions which may have their roots embedded in ancient beliefs. The earliest date yet recorded for a stone circle is about 2500 BC and the latest 1000 BC – a period of 1,500 years over which the stone circles were being built. The beliefs which led to their construction must have been of a compelling nature – witness the transportation of large stones from north Pembrokeshire to incorporate into Stonehenge and the many instances where the circles can be shown to have been sited on the fringes of prehistoric territories – focal points perhaps where groups could meet and discuss their differences and common interests.

Defining the henges

Although within the overall category of ceremonial circles those built of stone are best known, several other varieties exist. These include simple circular areas surrounded by earthen banks within which may be a setting of stones. Circles of spaced pits also occur from time to time, the pits occasionally containing the remains of a meat joint as an offering or sometimes a human cremation. Very occasionally, circular settings of post-holes occur which had supported timber uprights. Within these categories of ceremonial circle, and largely cutting across them, is the

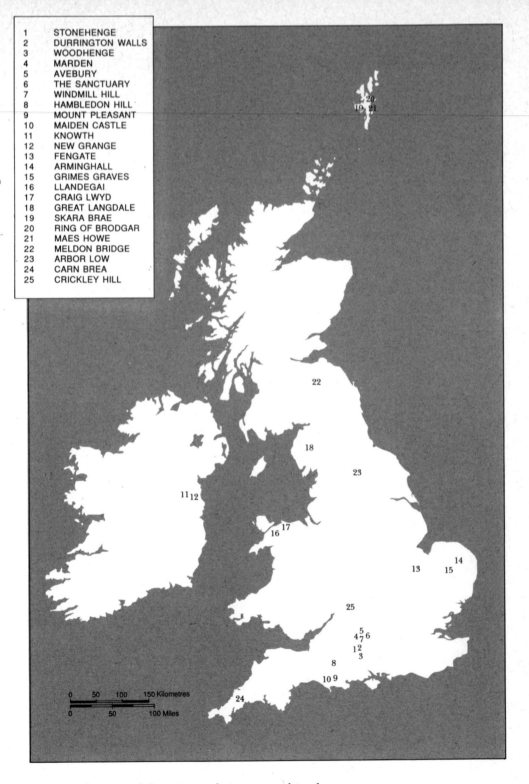

1	STONEHENGE
2	DURRINGTON WALLS
3	WOODHENGE
4	MARDEN
5	AVEBURY
6	THE SANCTUARY
7	WINDMILL HILL
8	HAMBLEDON HILL
9	MOUNT PLEASANT
10	MAIDEN CASTLE
11	KNOWTH
12	NEW GRANGE
13	FENGATE
14	ARMINGHALL
15	GRIMES GRAVES
16	LLANDEGAI
17	CRAIG LWYD
18	GREAT LANGDALE
19	SKARA BRAE
20	RING OF BRODGAR
21	MAES HOWE
22	MELDON BRIDGE
23	ARBOR LOW
24	CARN BREA
25	CRICKLEY HILL

1   *Distribution of the principal sites named in the text.*

group to which have been applied the name, 'henge' monument. This expression was first employed by Thomas Kendrick and Christopher Hawkes in 1932 who grouped within it a number of prehistoric 'sacred-places' which did not appear to be sepulchral. Strictly speaking however, the term should only apply to the monument from which it is derived, Stonehenge and its 'hanging stones' or lintels.

When Grahame Clark published the account of his excavations at Arminghall (Norfolk) in 1936, he appended a detailed discussion of henge monuments which he considered to be defined by a more or less circular area on which stood stone or timber uprights and which were surrounded by a bank, and usually a ditch, which was normally sited within the bank. Access to the interior was provided by one or two entrances. Clark also produced the first list of such monuments with their distribution, together with a list of enclosures which probably belonged to the 'henge' category but where internal structures were not proved.

In 1939, Stuart Piggott published a survey of ceremonial circles in Dorset and took the opportunity of sub-dividing the henge monuments into two classes on the basis of the number of entrances they possessed. The scheme had a monumental simplicity – Class I for one entrance and Class II for two entrances. In 1951, the publication of excavations undertaken on a series of henges and a cursus or linear enclosure near Dorchester (Oxon) provided Richard Atkinson with the opportunity of reviewing the evidence for henge monuments. The features which guided him in augmenting Clark's list were principally the surrounding earthwork with an internal ditch which was interrupted by one or more entrances and surrounded a circular area. The structures found within the bank and ditch were very varied and could include settings of stones, posts, pits or burials. Atkinson also confirmed the division of the henges into Class I and Class II and subdivided the latter group by the addition of a Class II A Type. The latter was characterized by two concentric ditches enclosing a single bank between them and limited geographically to the area between the Rivers Ure and Swale in Yorkshire.

A henge monument therefore came to be defined as a circular area of variable size enclosed by a bank and a ditch, the former normally sited outside the latter and broken by one or more entrances. Nearly 100 monuments of this class have been recognized, widely distributed throughout the British Isles from Cornwall to the Orkneys. Six areas show remarkable concentrations – the Salisbury Avon, the Mendips, the Thames Valley, Ripon in Yorkshire, the valley of the Boyne in Ireland

and the Moray Firth in Inverness. They vary in diameter from small monuments such as Fargo Plantation (Wilts) of 10.6 m to the great monuments such as Avebury or Durrington Walls in Wiltshire with diameters in excess of 300 m. Their internal and external structures are also extremely varied and in some cases none has been recorded at all. Where they occur they include stone and timber structures, pits and burials. Their variety is such that a single generic name for them no longer seems appropriate but the term 'henge' is now so hallowed by over 50 years of usage that it seems likely to survive until a better is devised. Of the 100 or so henge monuments in Britain it is apparent that the only feature which distinguishes them from other monuments of ceremonial circle type, such as Stanton Drew, Cefn Côch etc., is the presence of a bank and ditch. Their characterization as a separate category within the great range and abundance of monuments built within the ceremonial circle tradition is therefore based on the separation of the enclosed and therefore special area from its surroundings.

The variety of henge monuments

The four largest henges in Neolithic Britain are located in an area of southern England which is notable for the variety of its prehistoric monuments. The most westerly of the four – Mount Pleasant – lies on the eastern outskirts of Dorchester some 80 km south-west of Stonehenge. The other three from north to south are Avebury, Marden and Durrington Walls in Wiltshire. All are adjacent to the River Avon and within a day's walk of one another. The programme of archaeological excavations carried out at Durrington Walls, Marden and Mount Pleasant between 1966 and 1971 forms the basis for this account, although the sequence of fieldwork and research which constituted that programme had an origin in events some 40 years previously.

In 1925, aerial observation by Squadron Leader Insall resulted in the discovery of a series of concentric rings of dark marks where moisture had retarded the ripening wheat within a surrounding earthwork. The site was subsequently known as Woodhenge and is sited some 60 m south of the Durrington Walls enclosure. Originally known as the 'doughcover' from its domed profile, the earthwork had first been listed as a Bronze Age disc barrow, but following its discovery by Insall – a pioneer in archaeological aerial photography – the entire area within the ditch that surrounded the structure was excavated by Maude Cunnington between 1926 and 1928. The dark spots in the wheat proved to be six roughly concentric settings of post-holes arranged in an oval plan (marked today with grim arrays of concrete blocks), the outermost ring measuring 43 m by 40 m. The surrounding bank had been almost totally flattened by ploughing but had occupied an area 85 m in diameter overall, whilst the inner ditch was breached by a single entrance facing north towards the Durrington Walls enclosure. The name 'Woodhenge' was coined on account of the resemblances to the better preserved Stonehenge 3 km to the south-west.

The attentions of Mrs Cunnington were next diverted to the Avebury region in north Wiltshire where on Overton Hill there now stands a drab collection of modern concrete cylinders and slabs representing the site of a series of structures both of wood and stone that were dated to the late third and second millennia BC – and which have been named The Sanctuary. Maude Cunnington excavated this site in 1930, having located it on the basis of an earlier statement by the antiquary William Stukeley that it could be seen from the end of the Beckhampton Avenue close by Avebury. The structure was sited on a small level platform on the hill and, unlike Woodhenge, was re-built on several occasions, the

Colour plates *(pages 17–20)*

final reconstruction being in stone. It was not surrounded by a bank and ditch, but like Woodhenge, the timber structure consisted ultimately of six concentric rings of post-holes, the plans of which were based on true circles, not on egg-shaped rings as at Woodhenge.

A timber structure of rather different type was discovered from the air by Insall in 1929 at Arminghall in Norfolk. The excavation of the site by Grahame Clark in 1935 revealed that two concentric ditches with a bank between them enclosed a circular area some 27 m in diameter. This was occupied by a penannular setting of eight post-holes 14 m in diameter, opening towards the single entrance in the inner ditch. Each post-hole was approached by a ramp and the oak timbers were 1 m in diameter. Arminghall clearly represents a structure of different type from those investigated by Mrs Cunnington at Woodhenge and the Sanctuary. A diameter of 14 m, with no internal supports or related rings of post-holes, makes it unlikely that the Arminghall structure was roofed. Alternatively it may have been lintelled or the posts may have been free-standing and carved with figures and symbols.

In 1940 Stuart Piggott interpreted the structural remains at Wood-henge and the Sanctuary as a series of roofed buildings. There the matter rested until a fresh campaign of archaeological fieldwork which began in 1966.

Durrington Walls

The casual visitor may drive along the A345 north from Amesbury crossroads for 1 mile (1.6 km) to the enclosure at Durrington Walls, continue straight through the centre of the monument and arrive at the Stonehenge Inn without having seen any sign of earthworks to the left or to the right of the raised and embanked roadway. Yet the original dimensions of the monument when first built in 2000 BC were impressive enough. Its outer bank, originally 30 m broad and 3 m high, encloses an area which averages more than 500 m in diameter. Inside the bank, a level platform (the berm) from 6 m to 40 m wide extends to the edge of the ditch which was originally 16 m wide and 6 m deep. Some 30 acres (12 ha) of a dry valley descending to the River Avon are enclosed by the earthwork, but little of its former visual appeal is now perceptible. Millennia of ploughing have all but obliterated the bank, the ditch and the evidence for the two entrance causeways which formerly provided access into the enclosure in the north-west and the south-east from the direction of the River Avon. A spectacular view of the valley could

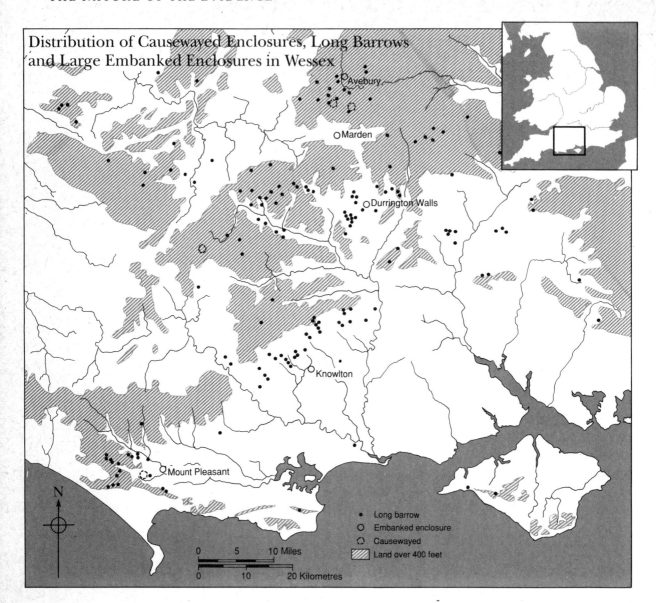

Distribution of Causewayed Enclosures, Long Barrows and Large Embanked Enclosures in Wessex

Avebury

Marden

Durrington Walls

Knowlton

Mount Pleasant

N

- • Long barrow
- ○ Embanked enclosure
- ◌ Causewayed
- ▨ Land over 400 feet

| 0 | 5 | 10 Miles |
| 0 | 10 | 20 Kilometres |

2   *Distribution of the principal Wessex sites relevant to the text.*

nevertheless have been obtained from the top of the bank and this may have been a factor in the siting of the monument.

In 1966 permission to build a road across the eastern half of the Durrington Walls enclosure from north to south was granted to Wiltshire County Council subject to a prior archaeological excavation along the proposed route. Archaeological excavation, which was begun in 1966 and completed in 1967, entailed excavating a strip that followed the line of the proposed road and included a part of the ditch and the south-west causeway. These rescue excavations revealed the post-holes of two circular buildings of Woodhenge type, which were dated by radiocarbon to the century around 2000 BC. Similar dating evidence and a type of pottery known as Grooved Ware – flat-based, straight-sided and profusely decorated with linear and curvilinear motifs – were obtained from the surrounding earthwork.

Marden and Mount Pleasant

As a result of the 1967 excavations a survey was made of enclosures similar to that at Durrington. They were not numerous and occurred at Marden in the Vale of Pewsey; Avebury (a monument already famous on account of its stone circles and avenue); and Mount Pleasant near Dorchester. Enclosures at Knowlton in Dorset and Waulud's Bank near Leagrave in Bedfordshire can probably be placed in the same category. Both the Marden and Mount Pleasant enclosures were in arable cultivation and it was considered that if post-holes of structures similar to those at Durrington Walls occurred within them, then they were in danger of destruction from plough erosion. Excavations were therefore conducted at Marden in 1969. The north entrance into the enclosure was investigated and a small circular timber structure recorded within the entrance in the same relative position as the large building at Durrington Walls. The earthwork was also associated with pottery of the Grooved Ware ceramic tradition and produced a radiocarbon date approximating to 2000 BC.

In order to complete the programme, excavations were begun at Mount Pleasant in 1970 and completed in 1971. As at Durrington Walls and Marden, the earthwork was associated with Grooved Ware and radiocarbon dates of around 2000 BC. Within the enclosure were the post-holes of a large circular building, comparable with those recorded at Durrington Walls and Woodhenge and also associated with Grooved Ware and radiocarbon dates of around 2000 BC. An unexpected discovery was of a massive foundation trench for a timber palisade which was built to surround the hill-top in 1700 BC at the same time as the now decayed timber structure was replaced by a setting of sarsen stones. The hill-top had been under plough for centuries and the post-holes of the structures were very eroded. Had this continued without excavation much evidence would have been destroyed unrecorded.

In order to supplement work at these sites John Evans and the author undertook a small excavation at Woodhenge in the summer of 1970 so as to obtain environmental and dating evidence.

Throughout the project, which *inter alia* covered a period of some five years from its beginnings at Durrington Walls in 1966 to its conclusion at the end of the 1971 season at Mount Pleasant, one was aware that broader issues were involved, separate from those of ceremony, ritual, orientation and lay-out, which at that time surrounded the subject of henge monuments. The enclosures were clearly grouped into a single category on account of their large size, consistent ceramic and lithic associations and remarkably close structural similarities and dating. They were also sited at focal points for territories that had been established for centuries beforehand and in the Dorchester area in particular, continuous settlement could be deduced from an early Neolithic enclosure to an Iron Age hillfort and into later periods. The development and nature of these centres was therefore of considerable interest from the viewpoint of our understanding of the nature of society in southern England from 3000 BC. The project was therefore concerned with themes of society and settlement and to appreciate this it is necessary to provide a background to the shaping of the south English landscape in the previous centuries.

CHAPTER TWO

THE SHAPING
OF THE LANDSCAPE

By 4000 BC the rich grasslands of the north European river valleys supported numerous farming communities who relied for their livelihood on the rearing of cattle, sheep and pigs and the cultivation of wheat and barley. Communities were organized in small villages characterized by long rectangular houses which served as a common home for both people and animals as well as barns for the storage of farming produce. By 3500 BC early farming communities were established in Britain and Ireland, and the transition from hunting and gathering groups to stable agricultural communities had begun. It is considered that this transition was prompted in Britain, as elsewhere in northwest Europe, through a process of acculturation or copying the successes of others. Some farmers in Britain would have been colonists – the seed corn and domesticated animals, pottery and farm equipment would have been introduced from elsewhere. The first agricultural communities in Britain probably did not have a sufficiently stable agricultural base to build permanent settlements and few traces of the earliest agricultural communities have been found. What little is known appears to support the view that the early farming population was living in small family units in dispersed farmsteads amongst an environment of largely untouched virgin forest. Unlike the grasslands of the Rhine and the Meuse, no timber-built villages have yet come to light and most of the evidence comes from the scientific analyses of peats and soils rather than from artifacts or monuments. Early pioneer sites have been recorded at Shippea Hill in Cambridgeshire and Broome Heath in Norfolk, both of which indicate settlement by early farmers around 3500 BC. It is apparent, however, that within a few hundred years these early agricultural communities had spread to most parts of Britain and Ireland from the south coast of Dorset to the northern and western isles of Scotland.

Houses

The evidence for houses and structural remains of settlements is out of step with what we know of the geographical spread and vigour of this colonization. A small rectangular house has been found at Fengate near Peterborough along with domestic and agricultural equipment – pottery containers, flint scrapers for preparing skins, a sickle blade for harvesting crops, a polished stone axe for felling or coppicing trees and a shale bead for personal adornment. Remains of rectangular houses have also been found at Clegyr Boia in Pembrokeshire and Llandegai on the Menai Straits. Further west, Ireland has produced two of the most convincing house plans from Ballynagilly in County Tyrone, and Ballyglass in County Mayo. The former was a rectangular structure measuring some 6 × 6.5 m with walls formed by radially split oak planks and with two internal hearths.

Agriculture and industry

Evidence for the cultivation of cereals comes from impressions of wheat and barley on pottery fragments, ploughmarks preserved below subsequent earthworks, flint sickles for harvesting the grain and flat stone querns for grinding it. The evidence of cross-ploughing beneath the earthen long barrow at South Street in Wiltshire and the recovery of surviving traces of actual fields beneath blanket peat in the west of Ireland has enabled the extent and impact of this early farming phase to be fully appreciated. The picture is now of a widespread and effective agricultural exploitation of the countryside as a backdrop to current and subsequent developments. Alongside this successful agrarian exploitation there is evidence for the centralized production of flint and stone for the axes that were so important for clearing the land and for some fine pottery that made its appearance in southern England. Flint was a substance much in demand for the manufacture of axes and other tools. In Sussex at Cissbury and Findon it was mined by means of central shafts and lateral galleries and transported to regions where the raw material was scarce. Sources of appropriate igneous rock were also exploited at Graig Llwyd in north Wales and Great Langdale in the Lake District and the products from these centres are found on widely dispersed settlements in Britain and Ireland. Ceramics were manufactured from the fine gabbroic clays of the Lizard Peninsula in Cornwall and the vessels from this source occur widely in South-West England.

A comparatively recent development over the past decade has been the accumulation of evidence, and hence an increased appreciation of, the extensive use of wood for structures, tools and weapons. The pioneering work in the Somerset Levels by John and Bryony Coles has been central to our recognition that woodland management – in particular coppicing and pollarding – was a craft widespread in Britain before 2500 BC. This work, together with that of Francis Pryor in the East Anglian Fens, has also rectified the imbalance in the archaeological record by recovering artifacts of wood, leather, rope and basketry. We now know that before 3000 BC a 2 km stretch of bog between the Polden Hills and Westhay Island in the Somerset Levels was bridged by a wooden trackway of pegged oak planks. It would not have been a complicated task to build the track but its existence implies regular traffic, the existence of settlements and the need to construct such permanent ways which had a value to the community as a whole.

Long barrows

Given this background of prosperity and a large and dispersed population seeking the best land and resources throughout Britain, it is perhaps not surprising that the evidence for change from 2500 BC took the form of social differentiation, status and the emergence of hierarchical societies combined with social conflict. This was preceded by a slowing down of the agricultural expansion which had been such a feature of the previous centuries. The tombs of the early farming communities were of a monumental character – long barrows that were often stone-built in the west and the north but elsewhere constructed from wood and turf. In Wessex, they were made of chalk mounds which covered wooden mortuary chambers in which were the remains of individuals whose remains had been allowed to decompose elsewhere in preparation for secondary burial in the barrow. Grave goods are sparse and simple and generally restricted to the normal range of artifacts of the period such as pottery, polished axes of flint and stone and chipped flint tools. It is thus fair to conclude for Wessex, as for the rest of the country, that the tombs did not serve for displays of personal wealth nor do the objects indicate that the dead were of high social status. This contrasts markedly with the situation after about 2500 BC which saw the decline of these monumental tombs and the cult of the ancestor and the appearance of single articulated inhumation burials. From 2000 BC onwards about 75 per cent of burials are in single graves and they also show greater evidence of social differentiation. A few individuals are accompanied by a considerable number of items. The single grave from Duggleby Howe in North Yorkshire was accompanied by thirty-three objects – the eight satellite graves in the same barrow had no associated remains. If one accepts a correlation between grave goods and status then the graves after 2000 BC reflect the emergence of a ruling class. It is noteworthy that many of the objects found in the graves are connected with dress since this is one of the most frequently used and visual ways of displaying and symbolizing power, rank or status.

By 2000 BC new objects used in burial rituals over a very wide area were beakers. These are finely finished red-coloured vessels with carefully executed decoration. The quality of the vessels is high and there can be little doubt that they represent part of a package of artifacts adopted by a small group in order to emphasize their rank and status. Associated metal objects, first copper, then bronze accompanied by gold soon increased in variety, and along with objects in other materials serve to confirm the emergence of a class society in Britain by 1700 BC.

Causewayed enclosures

A second type of community or public monument built by the early agricultural peoples in southern Britain was the causewayed enclosure. Most of the enclosures are roughly circular in plan and about 200 m in diameter, surrounded by concentric rings of ditches. The ditches are not continuous, they are broken by causeways and often contain the remains of 'special' deposits of food or human remains which were later covered by clean deposits of chalk or rubble. Over fifty such enclosures are now known from southern England. It is clear that both they and the long barrows date from the earlier part of the British Neolithic, 3000 to 2500 BC, and the former have been variously interpreted as settlements, cattle enclosures, ritual centres and periodic meeting places. A recently excavated enclosure at Etton in the Cambridgeshire Fens shows a differentiation between one part used for domestic settlement and the other used for burial. It is clear therefore that the enclosures served a variety of functions, some of which had a relevance to the community at large. Each would have entailed a considerable investment in manpower, they were sited in areas of productive land, some association with mortuary practice is a common feature and as with long barrows, their primary importance declined from about 2500 BC. There is some suggestion of occasional visits during subsequent centuries, but the motivation which led to their construction and the functions that produced the evidence for use which archaeologists have recorded, had both declined or vanished by the second half of the third millennium BC.

Fortified settlements

Perhaps the most striking evidence for social tension and the changes in society which became marked by the middle of the third millennium BC is the appearance of defended high status fortified settlements and the clear evidence for hostilities which accompany both them and other monuments. Such strongholds have been identified at Carn Brea and Helman Tor in Cornwall, Hambledon Hill in Dorset and Crickley Hill in Gloucestershire. They are sited on hill-tops and appear in positions chosen for their defensive potential. It is likely that more are masked by later Iron Age ramparts, or exist undated and not recognized for what they are. The excavations by Roger Mercer at Carn Brea indicate that prior to 3000 BC a massive wall of granite blocks was built. It was up to 2 m high and enclosed an area of over 7,000 square metres. Houses were built against the inside face of the wall to accommodate up to 200 people who lived there. The excavator has calculated that up to 30,000 man hours would have been needed for its construction.

Of the same age is Crickley Hill – a fortified promontory with long-houses arranged beside internal streets – and Hambledon Hill in Dorset. Mercer has shown that the rampart at Hambledon possessed a timber framework of a type more at home in the pre-Roman Iron Age. Ultimately the rampart was fired and bodies in the ditch – one with an arrowhead in its ribs – are explicit evidence for conflict. Similar evidence has come from Crickley Hill with concentrations of leaf arrowheads around the defended gateway and from Carn Brea. Elsewhere, isolated skeletons that show signs of a violent demise are testimony to the disturbed times of the mid third millennium BC.

It is also at this time that regional territorial groupings become apparent. These groups can be defined by comparing the spatial distributions of the different styles of pottery, of dominant axe types, the clustering of the enclosures and the designs of the tombs. From these patterns, we may deduce that regional communities were symbolizing their distinctive identities through coherent styles of artifacts or monuments. One of these regions was the chalk downlands of Wessex.

A time of change

The stability produced by the agricultural communities of the fourth and third millennia BC, their relative prosperity and communal reliance was clearly breaking down by 2500 BC. A standstill can be detected in the development of the agricultural economic base and in some areas it may have been a time of crisis. So far as can be determined there was little change in the climatic conditions prevailing at that time yet there is clear evidence for the regeneration of scrubland in some areas. In Norfolk, Suffolk and Wessex it has been demonstrated that land which had been cleared in earlier centuries for agricultural purposes was now infested with weeds and scrub. Even when such clear evidence does not occur, there appears to be some relaxation in the intensity of land use. The reasons for this are complex but are likely to lie in population growth due to the successful agricultural regimes of previous generations, coupled with the resultant loss of soil fertility as a result of intensive farming and the problems consequent upon these factors which would be connected with the political and ritual organization of society at that time. The latter can be seen in the decline of monumental tombs for communal, tribal or family use and the emergence of a stratified society exemplified by the tradition of single graves with differentiated grave goods, fortified hill-top settlements and the development of armed conflict between communities as a means of settling differences arising from problems associated with their previous success.

Out of this period of social change arose a tradition of monument building which had its roots in the past but is most plausibly to be viewed as a method of integrating different parts of an embryonic society in a single undertaking.

CHAPTER THREE

NEW PATTERNS
IN SOCIETY

The late Neolithic period after 2500 BC was a time of dramatic social development. Extensive evidence is now available for the emergence of regional identities and a number of core areas can be defined – the most important of which are Wessex, the Upper Thames Valley, the fen edge of East Anglia, the Peak District, the Yorkshire Wolds, the lowlands of south-east Scotland, the Orkney Islands and the Boyne Valley in Ireland. Some broad generalizations are possible – all are near the coast and they are all areas of outstanding natural fertility. Common traits were shared between the regions, particularly in respect of different types of monuments and the artifacts with which they were associated. In particular, Grooved Ware is found in all of the core areas. Richard Bradley has suggested that developments in the different core areas took at least three alternative courses depending on whether the major emphasis fell on a concern for ancestry demonstrated by collective burial, on ritual or ceremonial as with henge monuments, or on the particular individual as manifested by single burial.

Collective burial remained important in the Orkneys – although the tombs were more elaborate – and the Boyne Valley, in passage grave cemeteries where the local communities practised cremation. The persistence of the burial traditions sets these two regions apart from the others. The main regions where henge monuments played an important part were in Wessex, south-east Scotland and the Orkneys, with other significant groups in the Upper Thames, the Peak District and the Boyne Valley. In Wessex this in part took the form of the construction of enormous earthwork enclosures. Grooved Ware is found in all regions from the Orkneys to Dorset associated with henge monuments. At present, it seems likely that the Boyne Valley was one of the first of the core areas to develop a distinctive material culture with its great passage graves of Newgrange and Knowth. There are strong links between this region and the Orkneys which currently appear to show the earliest evidence for Grooved Ware and some of its associations – around the middle of the third millennium BC. In all regions substantial inroads had been made into the virgin forest that had awaited the early agriculturalists and a more difficult farming environment had been created. The earlier Neolithic populations had apparently exhausted their agrarian resources and the late Robert Smith showed this particularly clearly in the Avebury region. There are indications in this area that the heavily exploited clearings had not only merged, but suffered soil exhaustion and there are signs of soil erosion from nearby slopes. It seems probable that the most pressing problems facing the farmers were not only to maintain soil fertility but also how to combat weed infestation. Weeds, scrub and bracken are tenacious colonizers of broken soil and superficial disturbance is to them an invitation to proliferate.

By 2000 BC pollen studies indicate that many cleared areas were suffering from infestation by bracken, hazel and thorn scrub. New ceramic styles made their appearance – the flat-based straight-sided vessels of Peterborough, Fengate and Grooved Ware types replacing the earlier round-based forms.

Grooved Ware: origins and affinities of a ceramic style

Grooved Ware, with its flat-based bucket, or splay-sided bowl forms, carrying grooved or applied ornament, has no obvious ceramic ancestry, either within Britain or on the continent. It is, however, clearly established that by 2000 BC the ceramic tradition was used on ceremonial, industrial, domestic and sepulchral sites throughout Britain. Its essential physical characteristics are simple bucket, barrel, flowerpot and bowl forms, with profuse grooved and applied ornament arranged generally in geometric patterns with occasional spirals. There is also abundant use of relief ornament, although completely plain vessels are also found. Ian Longworth has defined four sub-styles in the Grooved Ware ceramic tradition, but with the exception of the Rinyo style in the Orcadian group, none shows any marked territorial separation. The tradition is widespread from Orkney in the north to Ireland, Wales and south England. The Clacton, Woodlands and Durrington Walls styles are essentially spatially interlocking and also occur in southern Scotland.

The only Neolithic villages with surviving structures belong to this phase. They occur at Skara Brae and Rinyo in Orkney, which were investigated over 50 years ago, and the Links of Noltland on Westray. All show the same type of cellular stone-built house construction set within a midden. Grooved Ware is present in abundance throughout the rubbish deposits and is thought to have developed around the middle of

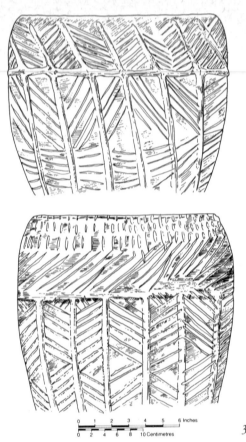

0 1 2 3 4 5 6 Inches
0 2 4 6 8 10 Centimetres

3 *The type of pottery known as Grooved Ware.*

the third millennium BC. In southern England Grooved Ware was associated with the major Wessex enclosures by 2000 BC, both with the construction of the earthworks and with the erection and use of the large wooden structures which lay within their circuits. Excavation of the flint mine complex at Grimes Graves in Norfolk, has similarly revealed that both the deep mining of flint and its subsequent processing at the surface are again the work of Grooved Ware users. The scale of the flint extraction industry is impressive. Shafts up to 15 m deep and 5 m in diameter were sunk through the solid chalk to reach the 'floor stone' layer. This contained flint of the highest quality lying in large tabular lumps. The floorstone was first extracted from the base of the shaft, then further quarried by means of radial galleries. A rough calculation suggests that just one of these galleried mines might have yielded as much as 40 tonnes of flint. The entire site could therefore have produced in excess of 28 million flint axes.

In Orkney, Grooved Ware also occurs in sepulchral contexts in Passage Graves of Maes Howe type, but unfortunately, elsewhere in the British Isles such detailed evidence for funerary practice is lacking. With rare exceptions, such as the settlements at Fengate and Hunstanton in East Anglia and the stake-built round-house with Grooved Ware beneath a barrow at Trelystan in Powys, evidence for domestic settlement is sparse and largely confined to pits, fragments of ditch and the remnants of occupation layers.

Attempts in the past to see an origin for Grooved Ware in the late Neolithic pottery of south-western, western or northern Europe, have failed to provide satisfactory prototypes for the main elements of the ceramic tradition. The total absence of necked round-based bowl forms marks a sharp break with both earlier and contemporary ceramic styles within the area of its distribution. Some minor decorative features can be ascribed to the absorption of native and Beaker traditions, but it is equally clear that the essential features of the Grooved Ware style – namely form, principal decorative techniques and patterns – cannot be so explained. The presence of applied decoration and extensive use of cordons is basic to this problem, for there is no satisfactory antecedent for these features in the known native bowl-forms of the British Isles. Ian Longworth has concluded that the Durrington Walls sub-style of the Grooved Ware ceramic tradition is a product which is native to the British Isles and that the major elements of its style are innovations which draw heavily on the skeuomorphic translation of basketry effects. The general scheme of a typical Durrington Walls vessel with transverse cordons with 'filled' panels, is essentially that of wicker basketry.

A further contribution to the tradition is that of Boyne Valley Art. The Boyne tombs of Ireland are the most impressive of megalithic passage graves which are distributed in four great cemeteries at Newgrange, Knowth and Dowth in the bend of the River Boyne; Loughcrew; Carrowkeel and Carrowmore in County Sligo. Grooved Ware has been found around the tombs of Newgrange and Knowth in the Boyne Group. One of the most remarkable aspects of the graves is the mural art which occurs on the stones of the kerb, passage and chamber.

The motifs consist largely of non-representational, curvilinear or geometric patterns – lozenges, zig-zags and circles. The tombs of the Orkney Group have also produced pecked and incised mural art comparable to that of the Boyne tombs. The grooved concentric circle and spiral ornament on four of the vessels from Durrington Walls and

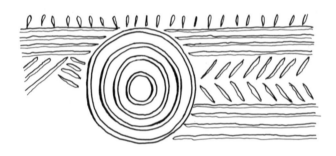

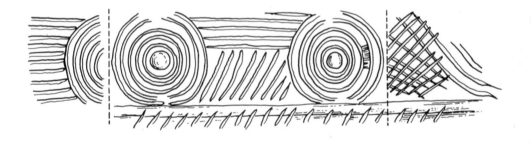

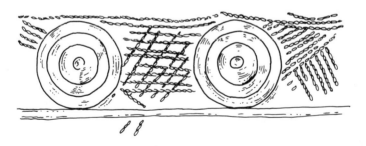

4   *Grooved Ware: spiral and concentric circle decoration.*

pottery sherds from Ipswich and Lawford in Essex suggest comparison with the art of the Boyne tombs. Other comparisons are with the three small chalk cylinders (the Folkton Drums) found under a round barrow on Folkton Wold in Yorkshire, which are decorated with curvilinear and geometric designs that find their closest parallels in Boyne Valley art, as do the highly decorated stone balls of north-east Britain, the antler macehead from Garboldisham in Norfolk and the two incised chalk plaques from King Barrow Wood in Wiltshire. Finally, the glorious spiral lozenge sherd from Skara Brae is so impressively matched in the Boyne Valley art style, that the integration of decorative styles seems an inescapable conclusion.

Despite the uncertainties which surround the Grooved Ware tradition and its origins, it seems clear enough that the four sub-styles were contemporary for much of their lives and that their origins lie around, or before, 2000 BC. The enigma of its seemingly abrupt appearance at this time without apparent antecedents, but with a wide geographical distribution throughout Britain and Ireland, remains unsolved. That sudden appearance is matched by the novel range of domestic, ceremonial, industrial and sepulchral contexts with which it is found and by the range of new artifact types which appear in the domestic assemblage. These include transverse arrowheads, polished discoidal knives and plano-convex knives of flint, incised chalk plaques and other

---

Colour plates *(pages 37–40)*

objects and a range of ornate bone pins. Bearing in mind that this new awakening is thought to have followed an economic recession in the later second millennium BC, the impression is given of a society strongly weighted towards a vast expenditure of human effort on the construction of public monuments related to ceremony, industry and, in Orkney at any event, the veneration of the dead. The distinctive ceramic style is found on sites of all types – domestic, ceremonial and funerary – and it is clear that it was not restricted to certain activities in this respect. It may be that it was the decorative motifs themselves which were significant. Some of them had wide currency and significance and occur not only on ceramics, but also on objects of the highest craftsmanship like the magnificent, carved flint macehead found in the Knowth Boyne Valley tomb, or the mural art from the Boyne Valley tombs and Orkney settlements and tombs. The designs may have had a special significance as part of a ritual which we have little chance of comprehending, or as a means of establishing group status. Certainly, the differences in the design structure on the pottery vessels represent synchronic variation, rather than change through time, which lends force to the theory that the new and powerful motifs served as identifiers of tribal groups.

Settlements and monuments

Increasing numbers of round barrows demonstrate the replacement of communal tombs with single graves, and displays of wealth and status through personal ornaments and fine objects found in these graves were supplemented by displays of power through the medium of monument building. Evidence for settlement is poor and its most visual manifestations confined to the Northern Isles where Colin Renfrew has argued that around 2100 BC late Neolithic Orkney may have seen the development of a more centralized society, the main physical manifestations of which were in the monuments, analogous in many ways to the developments taking place in southern Britain at around the same time. In Orkney the period is represented by the settlements of Skara Brae, Rinyo and Links of Noltland, the chambered cairns such as Maes Howe, Quanterness and Quoyness and stone circles such as the Ring of Brodgar and Stenness. All provide evidence for a subsistence base of mixed farming with cereals and the exploitation of game, birds and fish while Grooved Ware is plentifully found in the settlements and monuments. The Skara Brae settlement is situated on the Bay of Skaill and is a complex of stone-built houses and connecting passages built of the

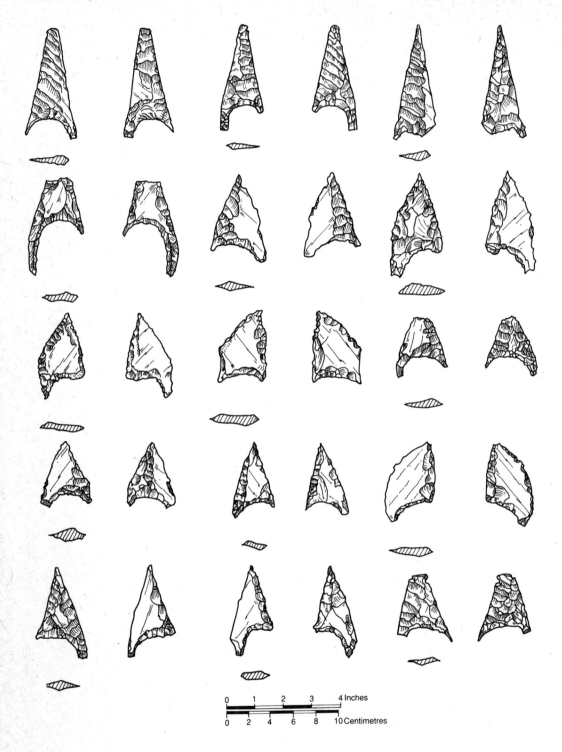

5   *Flint arrowheads from Durrington Walls.*

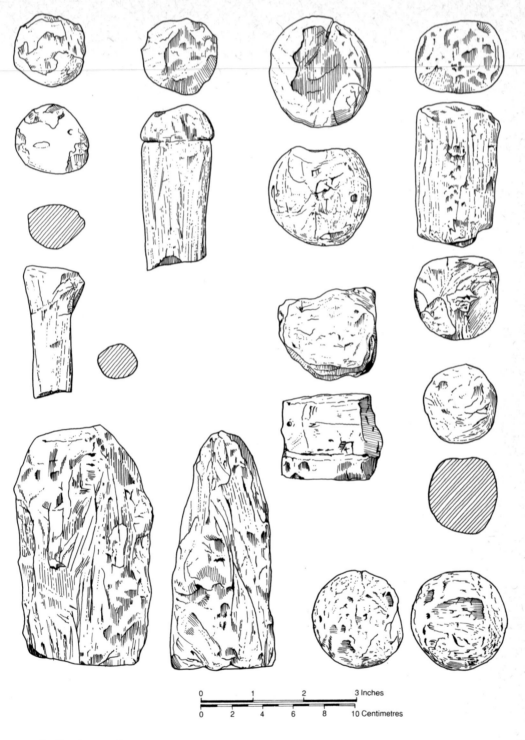

6 Chalk objects from Durrington Walls.

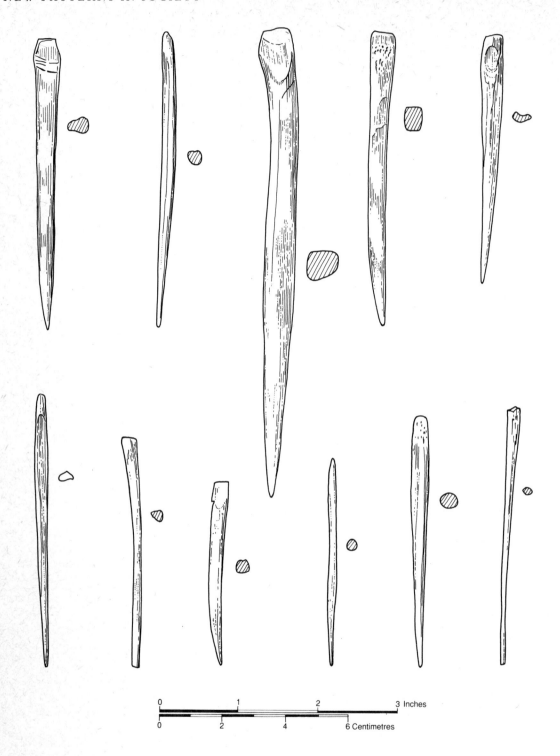

7   *Bone pins and awls from Durrington Walls.*

suitable Caithness flagstone. It was partially exposed by a great storm in 1850 and excavated by Gordon Childe amongst others, the most recent work in 1972 and 1973 indicating that the settlement was occupied from 2500 to 2000 BC. The houses were internally square with a central hearth and slab-framed beds and shelves. Eventually, the settlement became virtually covered by midden material and the houses were connected by narrow roofed-in passages. The most distinctive and widespread artifact found in the settlement is the Grooved Ware pottery. Other artifacts are pins, awls, needles, beads of bone and ivory and carved stone balls. A feature of the settlement were the engraved, pecked and incised symbols recorded on the soft flagstones of the houses and passages. The motifs include lozenges, chevrons and triangles. The most recent excavations have produced carbonized grain, the bones of cattle, sheep, pig, goat, dog and fish, whilst marine shells – particularly limpets – occurred in huge piles.

At the Links of Noltland on Westray, a village contemporary with and closely comparable to Skara Brae and Rinyo, but at 7 acres (2.8 ha), four times the size, was excavated between 1978 and 1980. Field walls were associated with the houses and evidence for ploughing related to the settlement.

In the south of the country the evidence is confined largely to scatters of pits, occasional post-holes and fragments of Grooved Ware with stone tools. An exception is the complete plan of a settlement of around 2000 BC on the Fen margin at Fengate near Peterborough. Francis Pryor has excavated a single house site, surrounded by a ring ditch and associated with stock enclosures and a droveway. A large assemblage of Grooved Ware and flints was recorded as well as the bones of cattle, sheep, pig and goat but the evidence for cereal cultivation was slight. Elsewhere, the only certain house structures that have been recorded were found by chance below two round barrows at Trelystan on Long Mountain in Powys. Two stake structures were associated with Grooved Ware and radiocarbon dates of around 2250 BC. There was no evidence for the economic base for the settlement and as the houses are so isolated there is no certainty as to whether they are a permanent form or whether they typify seasonal settlement at one extreme of the territory exploited by the community they represent.

Changes in the economy

It has been argued that some elements of the population in Britain at this time relied on pastoralism and did not grow cereals. Like all generalizations this is rather an extreme view which clearly would not hold for the Orkney settlements, although it could be sustained for Fengate. It is a fact that there is a general absence of grain impressions from Grooved Ware sherds but this need not imply that cereals were not cultivated and we should seek a behavioural rather than an economic explanation for the phenomenon. Certainly grains of emmer wheat, bread wheat and six-row barley have been found in pits along with Grooved Ware at Mount Farm and Barton Court Farm in Oxfordshire and Down Farm in Dorset.

Nevertheless, Robert Smith has drawn attention to a number of trends within the Avebury region data that are consistent with the idea of reduced dependence on cereal cultivation. Wild animal remains are more frequent on late Neolithic occupation sites than at any time before and the procurement strategy changed from selective culling of red deer to indiscriminate hunting. Sheep rearing declined in favour of pig keeping – a trend repeated throughout the southern chalklands at this time. It should be remembered that the environment had changed as a result of exploitation over the previous millennium. There was a good deal less woodland and many of the areas previously cleared for agricultural purposes were being colonized by bracken and scrub. Bracken is poisonous to cattle, sheep and horses, but it is also the scourge of arable farmers because the rhizome network of a single plant may extend over tens of square metres supporting hundreds of fronds and resisting extirpation. If there was a solution it was surely the rooting habits of the pig to whom bracken rhizomes are everyday fare. Indeed the late Neolithic trend by 2000 BC towards increased pig rearing may well have been largely determined by a need to reclaim land rendered useless for arable farming by bracken infestation. The construction of the massive new monuments that are shortly to be described must have imposed a heavy burden on the economy that could only have been met by storing food resources against the eventual demand. Pigs, by virtue of their short reproductive cycle and large litter size are prolific sources of protein and fat. They were ideally suited both to the prevailing environment and to the heavy culling rates necessary to support the temporary population explosions associated with the construction and use of the monuments.

A period of monument-building

For the late Neolithic period conspicuous monuments dominate the archaeological record at the expense of ordinary settlements. If, as has been argued, the mid third millennium BC should be seen as a time of retraction in the landscape, the closing centuries should perhaps be seen as a time of adaptation with a view to establishing an economy capable of operating efficiently in the secondary environments created by the extensive and wasteful agricultural practices of earlier times. After this phase there was renewed expansion and pollen diagrams indicate that by 2000 BC some of the derelict land had been reclaimed. So far as can be established this reclamation first occurred in the upper reaches of the chalkland river systems in Wiltshire and Dorset where the construction of the big monument complexes took place.

The monuments took the form of bank-barrows or long mounds, of which only 10 are known, and Cursus monuments – two parallel banks with adjoining quarry ditches – of which 30 examples are known in southern England. The Dorset Cursus is 10 km long and dates in part from 2500 BC. Finally, the henge monuments of various types were built, of which about 100 are known in the country. They form part of a tradition of constructing ceremonial circles of earth, stone or timber and are closely related in type to the 900 or so stone circles that are found throughout Britain and Ireland. Of these a group of enclosures in Wessex at Durrington Walls (Wilts), Marden (Wilts), Avebury (Wilts), Mount Pleasant (Dorset) and Knowlton (Dorset) are distinguished by their great size (in excess of 300 m in diameter) and by the fact that excavations between 1966 and 1971 at Durrington, Marden and Mount Pleasant showed them to surround large circular timber structures that have been interpreted as roofed buildings.

It was the emergence of these manifestations of centralized power in Wessex – the focus on the individual rather than the community, the concentration of personal wealth in few hands and the emergence of a phase of great monument construction after a period of inactivity and retraction – that has led Colin Renfrew to characterize the early second millennium BC societies as chiefdoms. In such a society personal wealth was accumulated by the head of the group or chief. This person in turn controlled the redistribution of goods and services, possibly through ritual of some kind. The societies are characterized by large communal endeavours in which the chief would control the deployment of labour. Each territory was served by a focal monument or group of monuments and it is now time to turn to those that were revealed in the programme of fieldwork between 1966 and 1971.

CHAPTER FOUR

THE MONUMENTS

The four largest henge enclosures in Britain all occur in an area of mid-southern England which is notable for the number of prehistoric public monuments of all types found within it. One of the four, Mount Pleasant, lies near the Dorset coast some 80 km south-west of Stonehenge. The other three are Avebury, Marden and Durrington Walls in Wiltshire. All are adjacent to the River Avon and none is more than 40 km from any other. It has been described in Chapter 1 how a re-alignment of the A345 through Durrington Walls led to rescue excavations there in 1966–67. The results of that work led to further work at Marden in 1969 and Mount Pleasant in 1970–71.

Territorial patterns

These great enclosures were focal points for groups of related monuments of sepulchral and ceremonial type which have themselves emerged by 2000 BC in southern England. The four territories within the Wessex region with which we are concerned are:

Stonehenge Which along with its avenue, cursus, the Durrington Walls enclosure and Woodhenge provided a focal group of monuments for the territory for upwards of a thousand years. This period of influence can be extended backwards to earlier periods by reference to the causewayed enclosure at Robin Hood's Ball and into more recent times through the Iron Age hillfort at Vespasian's Camp near Amesbury. Typically, the continuity of the area as a focus for ceremonial and sepulchral activity is very pronounced and can be duplicated in other regions.

Avebury/Marden These enclosures are best linked as a joint focus in 2000 BC with reference back to earlier but adjacent causewayed enclosures at Windmill Hill, Knap Hill and Rybury. Although excavations were undertaken at Marden in 1969 there has been no recent work at Avebury. Nevertheless, it can be demonstrated that the monument was developed further than Marden through the addition of a series of stone circles which are linked by means of the West Kennet

Avenue to the Sanctuary on Overton Hill. Marden lacks these later phases in stone which it is reasonable to postulate were preceded at Avebury by timber structures of circular form.

Mount Pleasant This enclosure lies on the eastern outskirts of Dorchester in Dorset with the Maiden Castle causewayed enclosure only 4 km to the south-west and visible across a broad valley. Another henge at Maumbury Rings has been known for some time but recent excavations by the Trust for Wessex Archaeology have revealed a second enclosure 300 m west of Mount Pleasant and on the same ridge, as well as the post-holes of a monumental timber circle on the site of modern Dorchester.

Knowlton Around Knowlton is a concentrated pattern of ceremonial and sepulchral monuments which are spread for 2 km along a terrace above the flat marshy valley of the River Allen whose headwaters are demarcated by the Dorset Cursus. Three enclosures form the nucleus of which the northern is the largest – 227 m in diameter. The other enclosures are small – one surrounds a small ruined church, and none has been excavated. The large enclosure and its fellows have nevertheless been included in this group on account of their size and proximity to related monuments.

The enclosures at the centres of three of these nuclei were excavated between 1969 and 1971 and a descriptive account of the results of that programme is necessary before moving on to assess its impact on our understanding of society and ceremony in south England around 2000 BC.

Durrington Walls

The large circular earthwork situated north of the town of Amesbury in south Wiltshire has been one of the more neglected prehistoric monuments, overshadowed by the visual impact of Stonehenge some 3 km to the south-west. Amongst prehistoric ceremonial circles Durrington Walls is uniquely sited as its bank surrounds a dry valley which probably formed during the last glaciation between about 30,000 and 50,000 years ago. Its plan is that of a nearly oval enclosure surrounded by a ditch with an external bank which excavation and a geophysical survey showed to be breached by two entrances in the south-east and north-west. The bank is sited on the flat ground surrounding the combe on its north-west and south flanks, probably as a result of the need for a level surface on which to build an earthwork

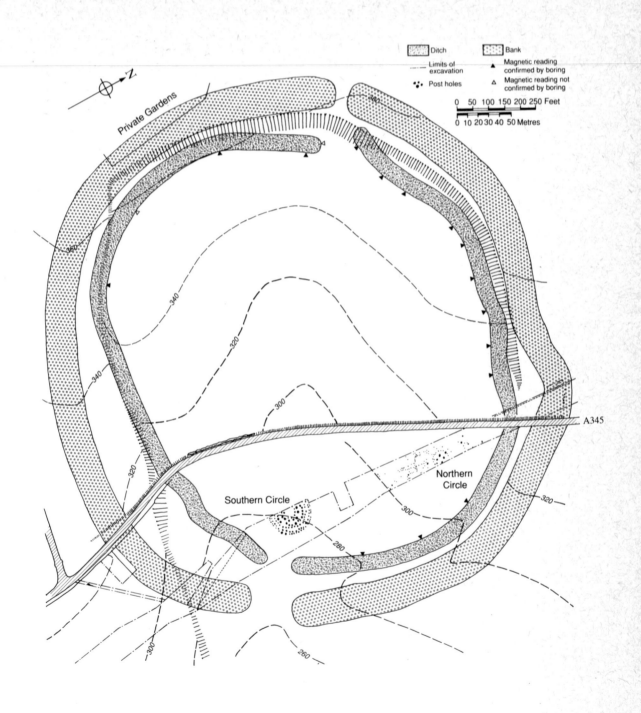

8 *Plan of Durrington Walls.*

about 30 m wide and originally some 3 m high. The enclosure has a history in antiquarian literature which extends back only to the early nineteenth century. Even then it is described as having been many years under cultivation and being much mutilated as a result. By the present century traces of the enclosure had been all but obliterated. However, a careful survey shows the enclosure to have been 487 m from south-east to north-west and 472 m from south-west to north-east measured from the mid-line of the bank. The west entrance is visible on the ground as a break 12 m wide in the low chalky mound which is the bank at that point. From the west entrance the bank is aligned in a regular curve around the west and south edges of the combe, keeping to the flat ground. At the point where it swings east the bank passes through some private gardens along the upper edge of the west lynchet, but thereafter it can be clearly seen under the right conditions as a low chalky mound into which the plough has eroded. East of the old road, the bank turns north down the side of the combe, where it is crossed by the south lynchet, to the east entrance in the floor of the valley where the enclosure most nearly approaches the river Avon. From this entrance gap some 38 m wide the bank swings north towards the old road and this is its best preserved sector where it is clearly visible, except when the corn is at its height. West of the old road the bank is again much ploughed out and is separated from the ditch by the north lynchet. It swings around in a shallow curve, always keeping to the flat ground, until it rejoins the west entrance. The interior of the enclosure is crossed from north to south by the old route of the A345 which has now been replaced by the new road on its embankment above the valley floor, which crosses a ditch terminal of the east entrance and then traverses the east half of the enclosure before emerging onto level ground to the north of the enclosure.

Centuries of ploughing have obliterated the ditch of the enclosure in every sector save the north-east, where it is still visible as a shallow depression. As a result, the most conspicuous man-made features on the site are the lynchets or cultivation terraces which follow the line of the ditch and which totally obscure the latter in the west and east. The combination of these agricultural processes and man-made features render the site much less impressive today than it would have been in the middle of the second millennium BC. However, although ploughing has resulted in the erosion of the bank and the chalk bedrock around the edge and upper sides of the valley, this process also caused the drift of a protective covering of soil onto the valley floor. Excavation revealed that in places this mantle of soil was in excess of 1.5 m thick and had preserved the post-holes of timber structures in the valley floor although those on the upper slopes were badly eroded.

THE EXCAVATION In 1966 the then Ancient Monuments Division of the Ministry of Public Buildings and Works was notified by the Wiltshire County Council of a proposed re-routing of the A345 road from Amesbury to Marlborough which crossed the east half of the Durrington Walls enclosure. An assessment was made of the possibilities of diverting the road elsewhere, but geological considerations made such alternative routes impracticable. Rescue excavations were therefore undertaken along the route of the proposed new road in 1966 and 1967. In 1966 the bank and ditch of the enclosure were excavated in their north sector where they were to be crossed by the route of the road. In addition, the bank was sectioned in its south sector and an area investigated to the south of the enclosure. In the following year, the strip of land which represented the route of the new road across the eastern half of the enclosure was excavated. It concealed the east entrance to the enclosure and the remains of important timber structures in the interior.

Before excavations began there were logistical problems to be resolved concerning the most appropriate methods to adopt in order to excavate such a large area 18–40 m wide and 762 m long, as it had been decided not only to totally excavate the route of the road across the enclosure itself, but also to investigate the area between the enclosure bank and Amesbury to the south, in addition to a slip road for Woodhenge. No excavations had been previously undertaken inside the enclosure, but it was considered to be a reasonable assumption in view of contemporary monuments in the vicinity that the hill-wash would have preserved important structures. Nothing less than total excavation was considered to be adequate and the problem of the removal of 1.5 m depth of plough-soil was overcome by the use of a fleet of mechanical excavators and dumper trucks – a daring innovation on the chalk of Wessex at that time. The disadvantage of such techniques is that objects in the plough-soil, whose distribution can add to knowledge, are lost unless they are seen at the moment they are uncovered. This loss, however, is more than compensated for by the extensive areas it is possible to clear, with no damage to any pits or post-holes that may have been dug into the underlying chalk. In the event the remains of two major timber structures were found. That named the Southern Circle was sited inside the east entrance in the bottom of the valley and consisted of a series of concentric rings of well-preserved post-holes with at least two major timber structures represented. This structure provided the most complex technical problems, for as a result of its position in the bottom of the valley the original dimensions of the post-holes had been preserved and were up to 1.8 m in diameter and 3 m deep in some instances, whilst the interlocking post-holes and ramps down which the oak posts had been levered made the excavation a complex matter. To the south of the junction of the old and new routes a second timber structure was found – the Northern Circle, comprising two concentric rings of post-holes approached by an avenue of timber uprights from the south. The erosion of the chalk through ploughing in this area had been particularly heavy and only the base of each post-hole was preserved.

THE PRE-ENCLOSURE SETTLEMENT The bank had been much eroded by ploughing, but part of its base was intact and had preserved a fossil soil beneath. On top of the soil and penetrating it for a distance of some 7 cm was a rich but localized deposit of refuse which produced pottery of earlier Neolithic type (plain bowls with round bases), flints (a polished flint axe and leaf arrowheads), bones and charcoal which produced a radiocarbon date of 2450 BC. The environmental evidence, based on an investigation of the soil profile preserved beneath the bank of the enclosure and on an analysis of land snails and pollen from the soils, demonstrates a distinct phase of prehistoric woodland clearance and possible cultivation prior to the construction of the enclosure. The original forest cover was dominated by hazel with a scattering of birch, pine, oak, lime and elm and was gradually altered to an environment of short turved grassland with a disturbance of the soil profile that could be attributable to arable cultivation. Such a sequence of environmental change has been attested from other locations including the companion monuments to Durrington Walls.

THE ENCLOSURE Immediately prior to the building of the enclosure bank the grassland environment, which had been maintained by grazing earlier in the third millennium BC, gave way to one of bracken and ferns. Whether this cessation is due to the enclosure of the valley it is not possible to ascertain with certainty, but it seems likely that the two events were connected. The bank when excavated was more than 30 m wide and preserved to maximum height of 75 cm. Originally it would have been about 3 m high and from its summit it would have been possible to look across the deep enclosure ditch and into the valley containing the timber structures. It would have provided a grandstand view of ceremonies in progress within the valley and Durrington is unique in possessing this facility which may have been intentional.

In 1967 the south terminal of the ditch at the east entrance was excavated and a 34-m length cleared to its rock base where a large quantity of pottery, stone tools, bone and antler of the late Neolithic period was obtained. Close to the steep rock face of the ditch terminal discarded refuse increased in quantity until it occurred in thick ashy layers against the steep terminal. The distribution of the material is entirely consistent with it having been thrown into the ditch by people standing on the entrance causeway. It had been dug from solid chalk with antler picks which were found sporadically on the ditch floor but near the terminal a pile of fifty-seven picks – worn and broken in many cases – had been discarded. Pottery of the Grooved Ware ceramic tradition was abundant, flint implements included an arrowhead, scrapers and a fragmentary flaked axe and three radiocarbon determinations dated the construction of the ditch to around 2000 BC. Its construction would have involved the excavation of 1,750,000 cubic feet (49,000 cubic metres) of chalk rubble with antler picks, baskets and ropes; the removal of the rubble from the ditch – bearing in mind that the weight per cubic foot of moist chalk is 1 cwt (50 kg); the transportation of 85,000 tons of this material across the space between ditch and bank, which could be as wide as 42 m, but never less than 6 m, and the dumping of the baskets of rubble on the bank, which was usually uphill from the ditch and which, when near completion, would have been some 3 m high. An estimated 900,000 man-hours were required to complete this project and to this must be added the task of erecting the timber structures within the enclosure. It is clear that the effort represented implies a society sufficiently stable and prosperous to be able to deflect such resources from necessities of food production and sufficiently motivated for the project to have been undertaken.

THE SOUTHERN CIRCLE   The post-holes of a complex circular structure, which has been called the *Southern Circle* were located 27 m north-west of the east entrance into the main enclosure. The structure was sited on a comparatively flat piece of ground in the bottom of the combe at the foot of the northern slope into the valley. The post-holes and their associated structures were excellently preserved by a deposit of plough-soil, 1.5 m thick, which had silted down the northern slope into the bottom of the valley as a result of centuries of ploughing and normal erosional processes. One can expect any other structures which undoubtedly occur on the valley floor to be equally well preserved although those around the brim of the valley were badly eroded.

Some two-thirds of the structure lay within the area to be covered by the new road and all the remains within this were totally excavated. In addition to numerous post-holes they included an entrance to the structure and a platform outside the entrance which produced the bulk of the numerous artifacts. That part of the structure which lay to the west of the proposed road was not excavated as it seemed desirable to preserve it for future generations who may wish to re-examine the results of the 1967 excavations. It became apparent as the excavation progressed that several phases of construction were represented and that the earliest structure on the site comprised four nearly concentric circles of slender posts flanked to the south-east by a façade of closely set timber uprights, which had been renewed on several occasions. When this structure had fallen into decay (there was no indication that the Phase 1 posts had been deliberately removed), it was replaced by a much larger edifice of six nearly concentric rings of more massive posts, the pits and ramps for which frequently intersected with the smaller post-holes of Phase 1 or destroyed them altogether. The single entrance faced south-east towards the Avon and was demarcated by two large post-holes outside which was a platform of chalk blocks and flint nodules. On this platform was an extensive area of burning around which was scattered a great quantity of pottery, flints, animal bones and antler. The preservation of the structures was so good that it was possible to establish the dimensions of the original oak posts and to determine the processes of decay.

SOUTHERN CIRCLE: PHASE 1 The earlier structure comprises four nearly concentric rings with an overall diameter of 30 m. The innermost ring was at the centre of four post-holes in a rectilinear setting. These post-holes are the only ones which were approached by ramps and they were renewed on several occasions. To the south-east the structure was fronted by a façade, 37 m long, which restricted access to the structure from the direction of the River Avon and the east entrance to the main enclosure. There is some evidence to suggest from the relative post-hole depths that posts of the façade may have decreased in size from the centre towards its extremities.

Not a great deal of human debris was associated with the structures of this phase – a few flints including scrapers and piercers, nine antler

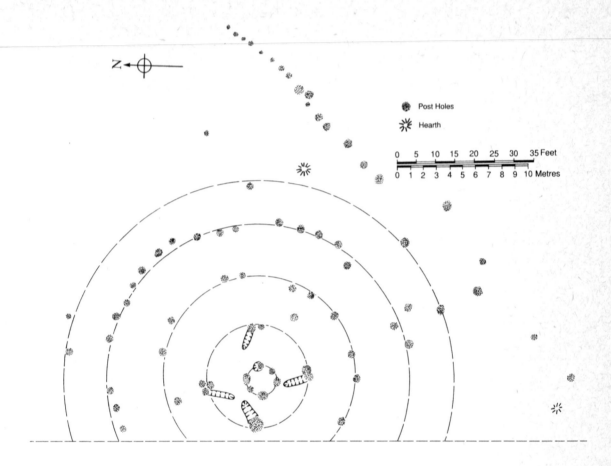

9 *Durrington Walls: plan of Southern Circle, Phase 1.*

picks, some pottery sherds of the Grooved Ware ceramic tradition, no bone implements and only a few splinters of animal bone. A radiocarbon date from fragments of antler gave a date of 1810 BC.

SOUTHERN CIRCLE: PHASE 2 In its second phase the Southern Circle comprises six nearly concentric rings of more massive timber uprights with an overall diameter of 38.9 m. Some of these rings correspond with those of Phase 1, the remains of which must still have been visible, either as hollows in the turf or as rotted stumps. The posts of the six-ring structure were much larger than in Phase 1 and required correspondingly larger post-holes, which were mostly approached by sloping ramps to aid the insertion of heavy timbers. The average dimensions of the post-holes varied between each ring, but the largest was 2.2 m in diameter and 2.9 m deep. They had been excavated into the solid chalk with antler picks which were then added to the packing material around the timber uprights. No fewer than 345 picks were recorded from the packing material of the post-holes and their excavation must have been a considerable undertaking, quite apart from the hewing, dressing, dragging and erection of the timbers to go in them. In general, the post-pits and the timber uprights they supported increase in diameter and depth towards the centre, but the innermost ring has deeply set, but relatively slender posts which contrast with the massive character of the outer rings. The entrance is located in the outer ring which faces south-

10,11   Durrington Walls: plan of the Southern Circle, Phase 2 (below), and the post-holes and decayed timber uprights (right).

Southern Circle: Phase 2

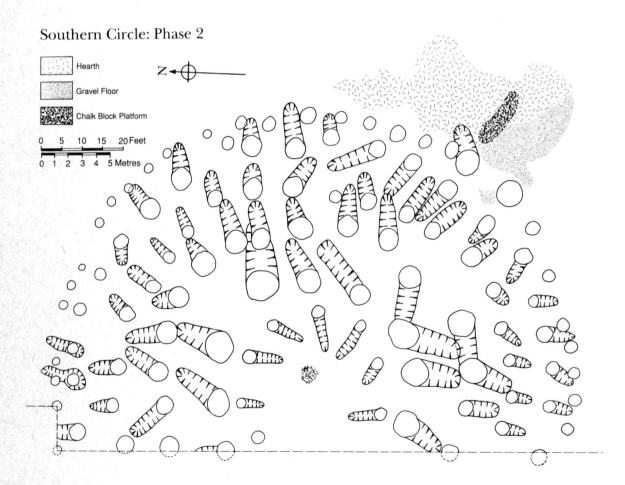

Hearth

Gravel Floor

Chalk Block Platform

0 5 10 15 20 Feet

0 1 2 3 4 5 Metres

east towards the causeway over the main enclosure ditch. It is 3.8 m wide and was flanked by two posts 1 m and 91 cm in diameter which are the largest timbers that were employed in the structure. In front of the entrance was an irregular platform of chalk blocks and flint nodules on which occurred an extensive area of burning which had scorched the underlying platform material and around which was littered a very great quantity of pot-sherds, flint and bone artifacts and animal bones.

North-east of the Southern Circle was located an elongated oval hollow 12.5 m long which was partly surrounded to the north and to the south by two arcs of stake-holes. It had been terraced into the slope of the hill and contained a black ashy soil with a quantity of animals bones, pottery and stone tools. Charcoal from the ashy soil, which in the centre

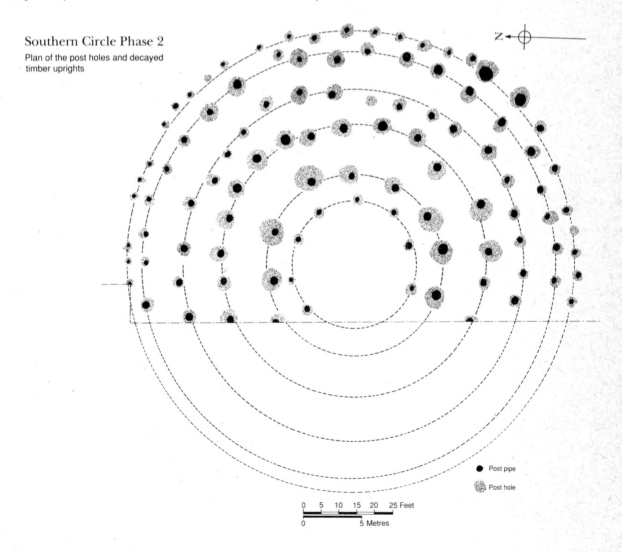

Southern Circle Phase 2

Plan of the post holes and decayed timber uprights

● Post pipe

Post hole

0   5   10   15   20   25 Feet

0   5 Metres

of the hollow was 30 cm thick, produced a radiocarbon determination of 2320 BC. The most probable interpretation of this structure is that it represents the remains of a midden, the rubbish having been thrown into a previously prepared hollow which was shielded by light fences to the north and to the south. Flint implements from the midden include scrapers and transverse arrowheads. Artifacts of bone include four complete and four broken pins and five antler picks. The collection of 981 pottery sherds is particularly noteworthy for the 25 sherds of Beaker pottery which comprise almost half the number of sherds from the entire site.

Returning to the Southern Circle, an examination of the charcoals indicates that the timbers were of oak. Only antler picks were recorded from the packing material and the pottery, flint and bone artifacts and animal bones were recorded from the bases of the depressions (or weathering cones) which had formed above each post upon its decay. In that sense the material is secondary to the structure but it is considered to have arrived in that position from having been deposited/dropped/swept or kicked around the post bases when these were still standing.

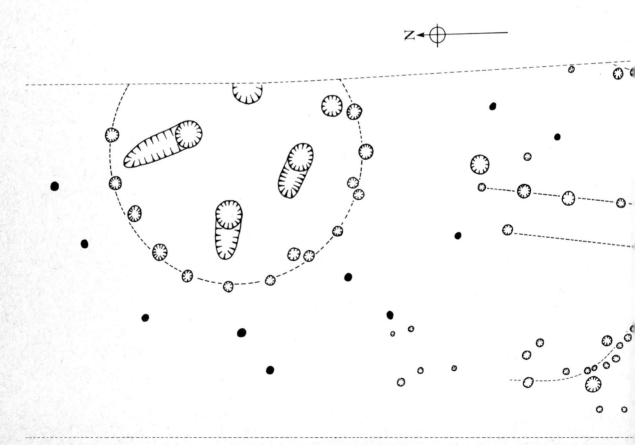

N

0   10   15   20   25   30   35 Feet

0 1 2 3 4 5 6 7 8 9 10 Metres

● ● Phase 1   ✿ ✿ Phas

Three radiocarbon determinations for Phase 2 of the Southern Circle gave a date of around 1950 BC. The structure also produced transverse and barbed-and-tanged flint arrowheads, flint scrapers, bone pins and awls as well as 345 antler picks. Only one axe was found – it was broken and of Cornish greenstone. It is clear from a study of the pottery that the Southern Circle was built and frequented by users of Grooved Ware and the great majority of the pottery was of that type.

THE NORTHERN CIRCLE The post-holes of this timber structure were located 121 m north of the Southern Circle on the northern crest of the dry valley. In this position it had not been protected by an accumulation of hill-wash so that in most cases only the very bases of the post-holes had been preserved and there was no indication of the diameters of the timber posts they had once held. In a number of instances the most shallow post-holes had been destroyed altogether and their existence is therefore inferential. Despite these uncertainties it was possible to establish the main outlines of a double circle of post-holes, approached uphill from the south by an ill-defined avenue which passes through a

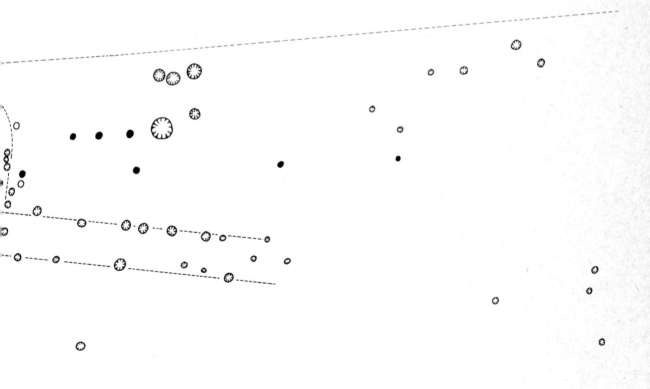

12   *The Northern Circle at Durrington Walls.*

protective façade. Approximately two-thirds of the structure were excavated, the remainder was outside the threatened area and left for the future.

There is a possible early structure on the site, but it is extremely tentative. The readily identifiable structure had an outer ring with a diameter of 14.4 m and an inner ring of four post-holes which are approached by ramps. In these post-holes the timber uprights had an average diameter of 59 cm. The slightly curved line of post-holes which formed the façade comprised closely set posts with a central entrance gap, up to which runs an avenue of post-holes and it was clearly designed to restrict access to the structure uphill. Some flint artifacts were recorded, two antler picks and Grooved Ware sherds. A radiocarbon determination of 1955 BC was obtained from an antler pick.

The data from these excavations took several years to assimilate before exploring the hypothesis that Durrington was one of a small group of key monuments for our understanding of the late Neolithic period in Britain.

Marden

The village of Marden in the Vale of Pewsey is built on a terrace of river and valley gravel which overlies the geological solid of Upper Greensand. North-east from the village the Neolithic earthwork was built on a floodplain sloping gently down to the stream which is an eastward flowing tributary near the headwaters of the Avon in the centre of the Vale, which at this point is some 6 km wide. The Vale is flat and marshy, particularly near the river bank and there are no obvious advantages in such a siting other than the proximity of the enclosure to a navigable waterway. About 16 km further downstream, the Durrington Walls enclosure is sited on the west bank of the Avon in close proximity to Woodhenge and Stonehenge, the latter having been connected to the Avon at one stage in its history by means of the Avenue. The importance of the Avon to the siting of these late Neolithic enclosures is thus made abundantly clear. To the north of Marden, a distance of some 11 km across the chalk uplands to the upper reaches of the River Kennet is the Avebury enclosure. Of similar dimensions to Marden, Durrington Walls and Mount Pleasant, Avebury is flanked to the south-east by the Sanctuary – a structure of complicated history which in its final timber stage was comparable to those structures excavated at Woodhenge, Durrington Walls and Mount Pleasant.

The purpose of the limited excavations at Marden in 1969 was to establish whether the enclosure contained timber structures of Durrington Walls type and if so, whether these remains were being injuriously affected by ploughing. The survey indicated that the bank with internal ditch occupied some 35 acres (14 ha) on the floodplain of the Avon, the internal dimensions being 530 m from the north to south and 360 m from east to west. The roughly oval area was therefore bordered on its south side by the River Avon with no sign of an earthwork on the floodplain. In addition to this access to a waterway, two entrances were provided in the north and the east through the bank and ditch. The north entrance was visible on the ground and excavation showed gaps of 15 m between the bank terminals and 10 m between the ditch terminals.

The east entrance had been obliterated by ploughing and was located in a geophysical survey and by boring, which showed the gaps between the bank and ditch terminals to be approximately 19 m and 14 m respectively. The earthworks have been mostly flattened by ploughing save in their north-west sector where the bank is preserved under woodland to a height of 2.7 m and width of 40 m. The terminals of the banks and ditches on the floodplain are clearly visible as earthworks and the enclosure is bisected by the road north from Marden. In the early nineteenth century a huge barrow was recorded east of the road near the earthwork and described as having an overall diameter of 160 m and a height of 7 m. However, by 1818 the Hatfield Barrow as it was known, had been completely levelled and its siting remained unknown until the geophysical survey in 1969 located its ditch. South of the Hatfield Barrow, on the edge of the floodplain, is a circular enclosure c.60 m in diameter which, like the Hatfield Barrow, was dug into in the early nineteenth century and some sherds and charcoal recorded.

The excavation in 1969 was limited to the ditch terminal and the bank terminals at the north entrance, together with an area excavation south of the entrance causeway in a successful attempt to locate timber structures.

THE PRE-ENCLOSURE SETTLEMENT Evidence for an occupation of the site which preceded the enclosure by some 500 years was recorded from the fossil soil which had been preserved beneath the enclosure bank. Within this soil at a depth of about 7 cm was a layer of flint artifacts,

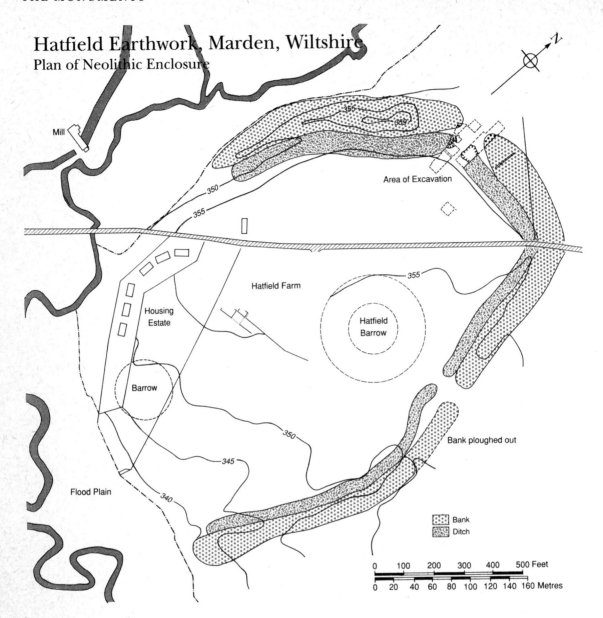

Hatfield Earthwork, Marden, Wiltshire
Plan of Neolithic Enclosure

Mill

350

355

Area of Excavation

355

Hatfield Farm

Housing
Estate

Hatfield
Barrow

Barrow

350

345

Flood Plain

340

Bank ploughed out

Bank
Ditch

0   100   200   300   400   500 Feet

0   20   40   60   80   100   120   140   160 Metres

13   Plan of Marden

pottery sherds and charcoal – the pottery being plain round-bottomed bowls of earlier Neolithic type. A radiocarbon determination on a sample of charcoal from this layer produced a date of 2654 BC, whilst the date of the construction of the earthwork is provided by a determination of 1988 BC from the bottom of the ditch. These dates suggest that there was a substantial time interval between the earlier Neolithic occupation and the burial of the soil by the construction of the earthwork.

THE ENCLOSURE The ditch and bank terminals were excavated as well as parts of the causeway between them. A 12-m length of deposits from the ditch in its eastern terminal was removed. The ditch was 16 m wide with a flat base 9.5 m wide and 2 m deep in the centre from the modern turf line. At the causeway the ditch expanded to 18 m wide and 3 m deep. Ground water occurred at a depth of 2.9 m and had caused waterlogging of the deposits and artifacts. The level of the water table early in the second millennium BC cannot now be established, but it must have been lower than at present, or else the digging of the ditch would have presented considerable difficulties.

The primary deposits in the ditch terminals on either side of the entrance causeway produced a quantity of human rubbish, the distribution of which is entirely consistent with it having been thrown in by people entering or leaving the enclosure. These deposits produced sherds of Grooved Ware and the associations of the enclosure are entirely with this ceramic style. A number of fresh, unweathered flint artifacts were also recorded as well as 34 antler picks and 6 rakes together with a quantity of animal bones. The skeleton of a young female adult was recovered from the ditch in a position which suggests a late Neolithic date, although it was clearly not deposited until some time after the ditch was dug. Three radiocarbon determinations were obtained from the bottom of the ditch and that of c.2000 BC on charcoal compares well with those from Durrington Walls.

Where the bank was best preserved, it was 13.5 m wide with a maximum height just short of 1 m. A small collection of flint artifacts was recorded from the body of the bank along with two antler picks. The entrance causeway was only sampled but produced several pits and post-holes, all of which contained Grooved Ware.

THE TIMBER STRUCTURE The post-holes of a circular timber structure were recorded 14 m south of the north entrance causeway. The subsoil in this area was clayey-alluvium, the surface of which produced scattered flint artifacts, occasional Grooved Ware sherds and flecks of charcoal and which was covered by only 21 cm of turf and plough-soil. The plan of the structure was simple and represented by a ring of post-holes some 10.5 m in diameter. The average depth of the post-holes was only 15 cm (max 30 cm) but the majority retained impressions of the timber uprights that they had once contained. Grooved Ware was recorded from two post-holes and an adjacent pit as well as from the surface of the subsoil within the structure. The flint implements include an arrowhead and scrapers.

14   Marden: plan of timber structure.

PLAN OF THE POST HOLES AND DECAYED TIMBER UPRIGHTS

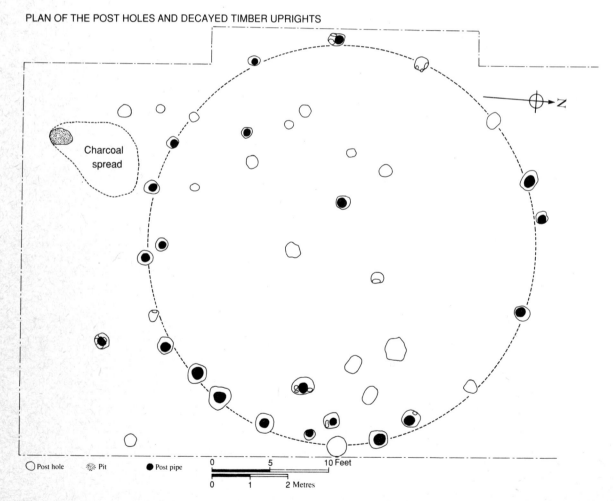

Charcoal spread

N

○ Post hole   ⠿ Pit   ● Post pipe

0   5   10 Feet

0   1   2 Metres

Marden had been selected for survey and excavation in 1969 on account of its similarities with the Durrington Walls enclosure, on the west bank of the Avon 16 km downstream, and therefore to establish whether the post-holes of any timber structures within it were being eroded by ploughing. As a result of the excavations the resemblances between the Durrington Walls and Marden enclosures were confirmed on several grounds. First, on account of the comparable size of the enclosures, with Marden being the larger of the two sites. Secondly, on account of the associated cultural remains, for not only were the enclosure and timber structure at Marden associated solely with Grooved Ware, but the pottery from the two sites shared many stylistic traits which provide a cultural and chronological link. This latter aspect was confirmed by the radiocarbon determinations from both Marden and Durrington Walls which dated both enclosures, and the timber structures within the latter, to the beginning of the second millennium BC. Finally, the simple post-hole setting within the north entrance at Marden demonstrated that this enclosure, like that at Durrington Walls, also surrounded timber structures and that the Marden ring had the same siting equivalent to an entrance as did the Southern Circle at Durrington Walls. These cultural, chronological and structural relationships, combined with a common siting on the waterway of the River Avon, indicated that both enclosures and their associated structures were built at the same time for similar purposes by people sharing closely comparable cultural traditions. The time was therefore opportune to undertake a project at the third of the great Wessex enclosures – which, like Durrington and Marden had not previously been investigated, to confirm the hypothesis that these enclosures, along with Avebury and Knowlton, formed a closely knit group and were important centres at the beginning of the third millennium BC.

Mount Pleasant and its region

The low hill called Mount Pleasant lies across a ridge on the eastern edge of Dorchester in West Stafford parish, Dorset. Distinguished by a copse of trees crowning the Conquer Barrow on the western bank of the enclosure which surrounds its summit, the original earthworks have for the most part been spread and flattened by centuries of ploughing. The single bank with its internal ditch encloses an irregular oval or egg-shaped area on a low ridge running east-west between the valley of the Frome to the north and the South Winterbourne to the south. South of

Mount Pleasant, the Winterbourne is barely more than a stream flowing through a broad fertile valley from its source south-west of the early Neolithic and Iron Age earthworks on Maiden Castle, which itself lies 6 km south-west of Mount Pleasant. The gradient from the valley north to Mount Pleasant hill is gentle, but the latter is still a prominent feature when seen from the bank of the stream. North of the hill, the ground slopes steeply to the River Frome, which lies in its broad valley some 250 m distant. To the south the hill is bounded by the Dorchester-Wareham road (A352) and the minor road which leads to West Stafford village; while at the foot of the steep slope to the north is the railway track and cutting which serves those same towns. The western edge of the enclosure is bounded by the Came View housing estate, the gardens of which have encroached on the western slopes of the Conquer Barrow. From the summit of the hill looking east one can identify the low ridge which must have provided the easiest access route and on whose axis were sited successive entrances into the prehistoric enclosures. The enclosure is crossed by a hedge-bank from east to west and the area enclosed by the eroded earthworks is egg-shaped, with overall dimensions in the order of 370 m from west to east and 320 m from north to south. The earthworks are best preserved in their southern sector where it can be seen that the bank is external, interrupted by an entrance 32 m wide. On its western perimeter the enclosure bank is crowned by the Conquer Barrow which is a large though somewhat disturbed mound, still standing 3–4 m high on a linear earthwork surviving to a height of 4 m, which presumably represents the original height of the Neolithic bank when the barrow was built.

The preservation of the bank under the Conquer Barrow serves to emphasize the destruction elsewhere. Elsewhere, at best, it survives to a height of only 1.5 m as a spread of chalk rubble 16–18 m wide in the plough-soil. Within the bank is the ditch which is normally some 17 m wide. To the east of the south-east entrance the bank can be traced on the ground around the eastern perimeter of the enclosure where a second entrance gap 32 m wide occurs on the axis of the ridge. To the north of the hedge-line, all traces of the bank soon vanish, geophysical survey confirmed the entrances in the east and south-east, but also recorded unsuspected entrances through the ditch in the west and north. The line of the ditch was also established without question around the hill-top and a subsidiary ditched enclosure, previously only recorded on aerial photographs, was located south of the summit. Finally, the surveys located and planned a previously unsuspected feature – a foundation

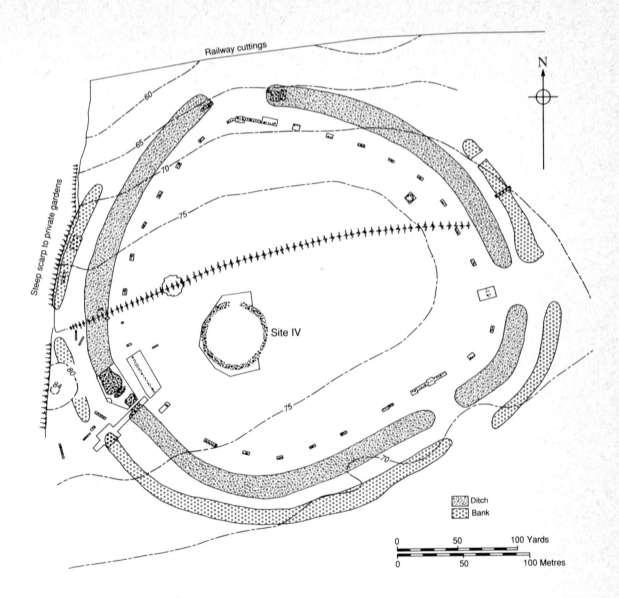

15   *Plan of Mount Pleasant.*

trench for a timber wall 1–2 m wide and 3 m deep, which surrounded the whole hill-top. Visual inspection, geophysical aids and aerial photographs therefore established that the 12-acre (4.8-ha) enclosure was surrounded by a bank and internal ditch which was breached by four entrances. Within the ditch and also surrounding the hill-top was a substantial palisade trench, while south-west of the enclosure centre was a large ring ditch.

No excavations had been carried out within the enclosure prior to 1970 and no chance finds recorded. The excavations which were undertaken in 1970 and 1971 had, as their general objective, the clarification of the presumed relationship between Mount Pleasant and the Durrington Walls and Marden enclosures. To achieve this it was necessary to determine the ceramic and lithic associations of the enclosure, supported if possible by radiocarbon dates, and also to ascertain whether the enclosure surrounded a timber structure similar to those already recorded at those two enclosures.

THE PRE-ENCLOSURE SETTLEMENT The poorly preserved bank provided few opportunities for investigating the character of the fossil soil preserved beneath it. Where it was preserved, the molluscan fauna reflects an environment of dry grassland at the time it was buried by the bank. Artifacts from the buried soil include sherds of plain Neolithic bowls, a flake from a polished flint axe and two transverse arrowheads. Bones of cattle and sheep were found along with hazelnuts and a radiocarbon date of 2122 BC. Similar evidence for pre-enclosure occupation recorded from Durrington Walls and Marden indicates that settlement in Britain during the third millennium BC was more extensive than might be supposed from the comparatively rare monuments that have survived. Monuments contemporary with the pre-enclosure settlement at Mount Pleasant are represented by the causewayed camp and bank barrow on Maiden Castle hill south-west across the Winterbourne valley.

THE TIMBER STRUCTURE: SITE IV Prior to the excavations of 1970 the only structure identified on the hill within the earthwork enclosure was a circular ditch, visible on air photographs, which in the past had been interpreted as a barrow ditch. In 1969 this ditch was located precisely by means of a geophysical survey and in 1970 was totally excavated. It was sited to the south of the highest part of the hill on gently sloping ground between the 77 m and 79 m contours. When the surface of the chalk had been cleaned with trowels the remains of a circular timber structure were revealed, represented by five concentric rings of post-holes with a diameter of 38 m for the outer ring and 12.5 m for the inner. The very regular layout was designed around four corridors which divide the rings into arcs. The structure was surrounded by a ditch 3–4 m wide and 2 m deep which enclosed a circular area 43 m in diameter. The bank appears to have been external and a single causeway 7.5 m wide was

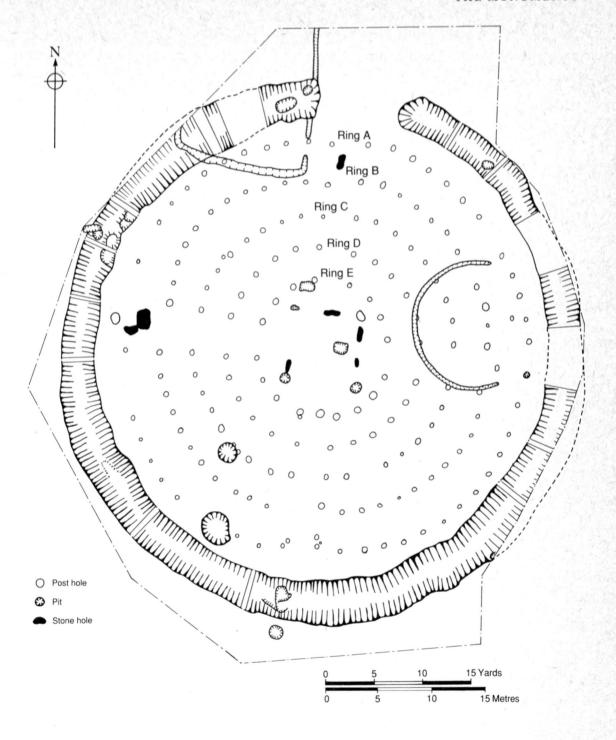

N

Ring A

Ring B

Ring C

Ring D

Ring E

○ Post hole

✸ Pit

◖ Stone hole

| 0 | 5 | 10 | 15 Yards |
| 0 | 5 | 10 | 15 Metres |

16   *Mount Pleasant: plan of Site IV.*

provided in the north. Three radiocarbon dates from the bottom of the ditch assign the construction of the latter to around 2000 BC. Pottery of the Grooved Ware ceramic style was associated with this ditched structure as were flint scrapers, a chalk ball, eleven antler picks, the tip of a bone pin and bones of cattle, sheep, dog, red deer, fox and bird. The chalk rubble silting in the bottom of the ditch was sealed by a fossil soil, the molluscan fauna from which indicates woodland conditions. Charcoals of hazel, yew and field maple were found in the chalk rubble and buried soil.

When the ditch was approximately one-third full of silt and a fossil soil had formed, the timber structure was replaced around 1700 BC by a central setting of pits and sarsen monoliths arranged around three sides of a rectangle. The siting of this structure implies that the ground plan at least of the earlier timber uprights was known – if only represented by rotting posts. Outlying pits and monoliths were recorded to the west, north and east. Pottery from the ditch deposits contemporary with the construction of the stone monument includes Grooved Ware and beaker sherds whilst fragments of Bronze Age pottery (Food vessels and Collared Vessels) came from the later silts. Other artifacts include about 3,000 worked flints comprising both transverse and barbed-and-tanged arrowheads, antler picks and spatulae and 300 lb (136 kg) of fresh sarsen flakes with a few stone mauls or hammerstones. These are presumed to have been derived from the preparation of the sarsen monoliths for the stone setting and outliers. The flakes are quite fresh and many have a percussion bulb preserved on them. The sarsens could have been derived from an original capping of Eocene sediments on the hill, traces of which occur in solution pits in the chalk. Alternatively, they could have been derived from deposits of Bagshot Beds nearby. The animal bones from the ditch deposits of this phase comprise cattle, sheep, pig, dog, red deer and birds and a single radiocarbon date assigns the event to around 1700 BC.

The stone structure was destroyed when the monoliths were broken up, probably to facilitate the cultivation of the hill-top in the first century BC. Iron Age settlement of this date on the site is represented by a gully partially defining a circular house 11 m in diameter and by associated pits. It seems likely that at this time the sarsen structure was demolished and its obliteration some 2,000 years ago, so that no visible record remained, is a salutary reminder of the incomplete nature of megalithic structures as evidenced by surface remains.

The structure (Site IV) is sited some 60 m from the main enclosure ditch at the west entrance. The inner edge of the ditch describes an almost perfect circle with a radius of 21.5 m. It was crossed by a single causeway in the north, some 7.5 m wide between the ditch terminals, facing in the direction of the contemporary north entrance into the main enclosure and the River Frome. No pits or post-holes were recorded on the causeway but the west ditch terminal was particularly rich in artifacts and refuse. The bank had been totally removed by ploughing but is assumed to have been external. The date of the ditch was established by three radiocarbon dates from its base of around 2000 BC and the associated pottery was principally of the Grooved Ware ceramic tradition.

The post-hole settings within the ditch consist essentially of five rings, the outermost having a maximum diameter of 38 m. The design of the structure is very regular and is based around four corridors aligned north, south, east and west, which divide the rings into four quadrants. The four arcs comprising each ring invariably possess the same number of post-holes – some of which had been replaced during the life of the structure. The post-hole sequences in the rings are fairly complete and the regularity of the latter enabled the missing post-holes to be estimated with a reasonable degree of accuracy. Because of erosion, the dimensions of the post-holes cannot be regarded as being relevant to their original size. Finds from the post-holes were very few and are confined in the main to 279 flint artifacts which include three scrapers. Sherds of Grooved Ware were recorded from fourteen post-holes and one half of a ring or pendant of fine-grained quartzite was recorded from a post-hole flanking the north entrance.

The timber structure was replaced by a central setting of pits and sarsen monoliths, with similar pits or uprights outlying to the west, north and east, at a stage in the history of the site when the ditch was approximately one-third full of silt and soil had formed over its contents. On top of this buried soil, whose molluscan fauna indicates a woodland environment, had formed a pale loam which at various points in the ditch circuit contained at its base an extensive spread of ash and charcoal, fresh sarsen flakes, stone mauls, flint artifacts, animal bones and numerous sherds of Beaker pottery. Charcoal from this deposit provided a radiocarbon determination of around 1700 BC. The sudden appearance in the ditch silts of such large quantities of knapped fresh sarsen flakes is taken to indicate the erection of stone monoliths within the ditched area. The central structure was based around four pits set on the corners of a 6 m square. The sockets for four sarsen uprights were

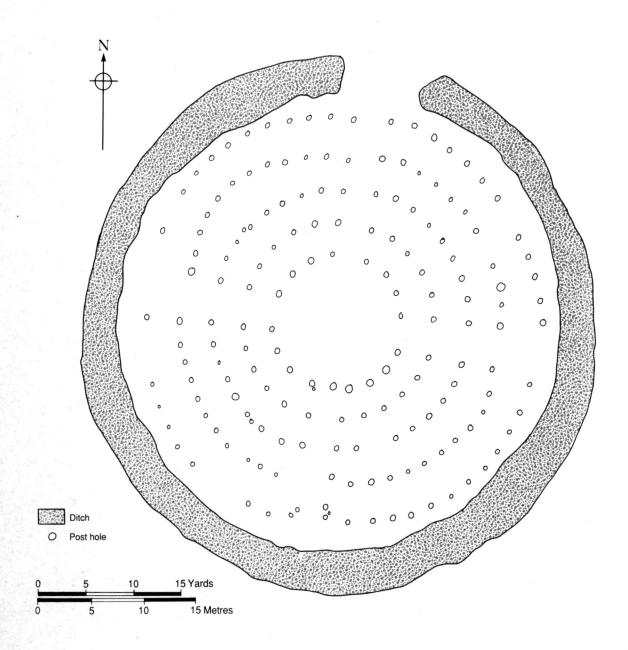

17   Site IV, Phase 1 at Mount Pleasant.

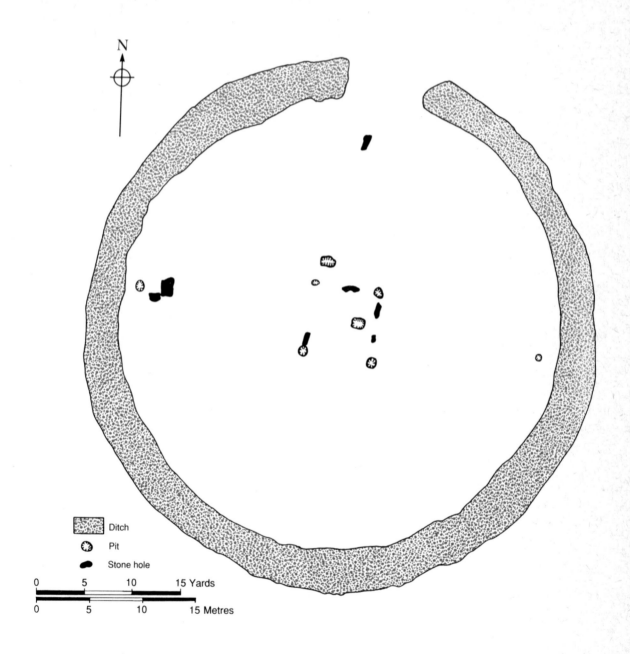

18   Site IV, Phase 2 at Mount Pleasant.

N

Ditch

Pit

Stone hole

| 0 | 5 | 10 | 15 Yards |
| 0 | 5 | 10 | 15 Metres |

recorded along the west, north and east sides of this square. They contained numerous fresh sarsen flakes, indicating that monoliths which they originally supported had been broken up *in situ* and in one socket was found the actual stump of the original stone. No sockets were recorded along the southern side of the square.

Outlying the central structure are two pits sited approximately on the line of the outer post-hole ring. Adjacent to the west pit were the sockets for two sarsen monoliths and another such socket was recorded to the north, just within the entrance causeway. There was no socket adjacent to the east pit but a concentration of sarsen flakes in the ditch at that point indicates its former presence. Finds were few and confined to flint flakes and sherds of Grooved Ware.

THE EARTHWORK ENCLOSURE The earthwork enclosure is of egg-shaped plan with overall dimensions of 370 m from west to east and 340 m from north to south. Of the four entrances, two in the south-east and east can be seen on the ground, whilst those in the west and north were discovered as a result of the geophysical survey. The bank has been totally destroyed around the northern perimeter of the enclosure especially where the ground falls steeply towards the River Frome. At the north entrance, there is a strip rather less than 25 m wide between the ditch and the railway cutting, where the ground falls away sharply at an incline of 1 in 4. The bank must have been built on this very steep slope and been very unstable, unless there was an effective revetment. A large area was excavated around the west entrance in 1970 with a view to removing the deposits from both ditch terminals and examining the causeway in between them. The ditch was extremely irregular and consisted of a series of intersecting pits, interspersed with unexcavated spurs and ridges of natural chalk. The deposits in the ditch showed a degree of consistency with a coarse chalk rubble at the base, overlain by a weathered horizon which in turn was sealed by a thick aeolian sediment and a plough-wash.

The causeway between the ditch terminals averaged 5 m wide and adjacent to it the ditch terminals were more regular, 7 m wide and 3.2 m deep with a flat base. Two antler picks were selected for radiocarbon dating. They were obtained from the floor of the ditch on either side of the entrance causeway and had probably been used in construction work. Both produced dates approximating to 1800 BC.

The most notable find was a flanged bronze axe which came from the north terminal of the ditch, 10 cm above its floor on the surface of a lens

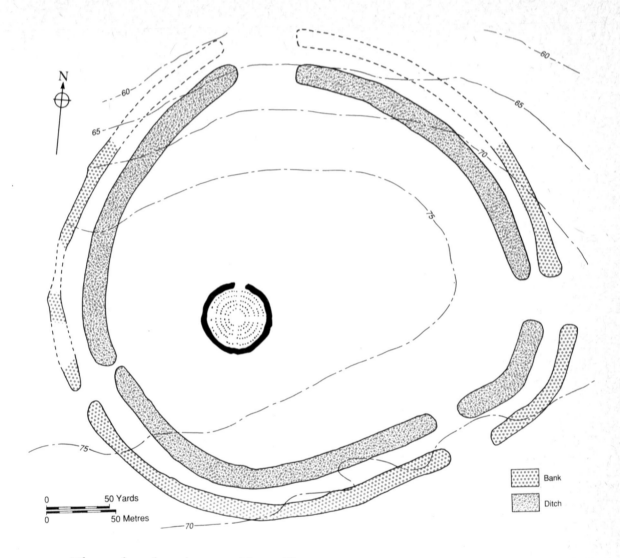

19   *The earthwork enclosure at Mount Pleasant.*

of chalk rubble. It was complete and intact with a thin butt and splayed cutting edge. Most of each face is covered by incised decoration of the kind sometimes called 'rain-pattern'. This consists of elongated indentations oriented more or less vertically and set close together. Such axes are characteristic of the Early Bronze Age in the British Isles and are often regarded as one of the criteria by which that period may be defined. It is, however, extremely rare for such artifacts to be recorded in the course of an excavation.

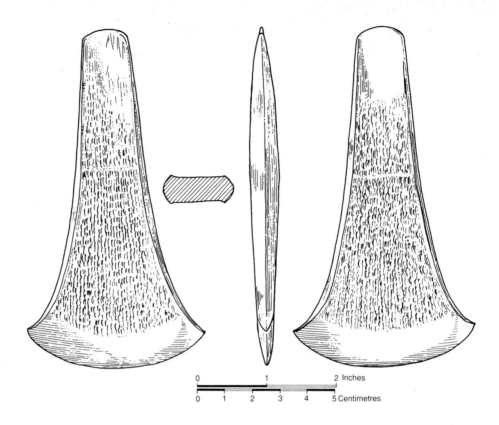

0 Inches 1 2

0 Centimetres 1 2 3 4 5

20 *The flanged bronze axe from the Mount Pleasant ditch.*

Although 1,570 flint artifacts were recorded from the deposits of the west entrance as a whole, very few were obtained from the primary rubble. These include flakes, cores, scrapers and one transverse arrowhead. A single phallus and a chalk ball were recorded in close association from the floor of the ditch to the south of the causeway. Twelve antler picks were recorded and animal bones representing pig, cattle, sheep, horse, dog and red deer.

The primary silts of the ditch terminals at the west entrance produced little material which could be used to determine the cultural context of the enclosure. In 1971 the north entrance into the enclosure was excavated so as to augment that evidence. The ditch terminals at the north entrance were also irregular and were between 2.2 m and 2.7 m deep. The east ditch terminal in particular comprised a series of broad shallow bays the largest of which was partially surrounded by large stake-holes. Two infant burials were also recorded at the same level. These hollows in the ditch floor provided shelter for several centuries when the ditch was slowly filling with silt and the deposits produced a succession of stratified cultural material and a sequence of radiocarbon samples which date from 2100 BC. These dates are older by some 200–300 years than those obtained from the floor of the ditch at the west entrance. The north entrance causeway is some 40 m wide compared with 5 m at the west entrance and the latter is crudely dug with an unfinished appearance. One may conclude that the ditch terminals at the west entrance were extended around 1800 BC resulting in their unfinished appearance and the reduction of the entrance causeway to its present 5 m width. The radiocarbon dates from the north entrance therefore, more accurately date the construction of the main enclosure ditch to the century before 2000 BC.

Only Grooved Ware sherds occurred in the primary silts of the ditch where they were associated with flint artifacts, antler picks and chalk artifacts including two fragments of a phallus. Animal bones include the remains of pig, cattle and red deer. In the overlying deposit Beaker sherds appear alongside Grooved Ware for the first time, along with a radiocarbon date of 1941 BC, flint and chalk artifacts and bones of pig, sheep and cattle. Some stakes had been driven into the ditch floor from this level, but these were most common when dug from the overlying layer which is also contemporary with the two crouched infant burials. A radiocarbon determination of 1669 BC was obtained from this layer which, in turn, was overlaid by a thick deposit of ashy grey soil which produced a quantity of pottery, stone tools and animal bones in addition to a radiocarbon date of 1509 BC. From the later deposits sherds of Bronze Age fabric begin to occur alongside the Grooved Ware and Beaker sherds with a radiocarbon date of 1556 BC and a segmented bone toggle. A cylindrical bone bead, decorated with geometric patterns was also recorded. It is rare to obtain such a well-dated sequence of ceramic styles which show that the main enclosure (and the Site IV ditch) were constructed by Grooved Ware users around 2000 BC. It is worthy of note however, that Grooved Ware continued to be incorporated into the silts high in the main enclosure ditch sequence to be joined first by Beaker and then by later Bronze Age wares. If this survival of Grooved Ware is taken to indicate continuity in the utilization of the site then it seems likely that the users of these later styles took part in that utilization and that the enclosure retained its interest for the greater part of 500 years.

A major achievement by John Evans was an analysis of numerous samples of molluscan fauna from the ditch silts. The land mollusca from a buried soil horizon above the primary fill at the west entrance indicate a shaded environment with a high relative humidity in 1800 BC, which Evans argues applied to the whole site. A major clearance phase which follows this was represented by a deposit of chalk scree which sealed the buried soil and which is associated with a radiocarbon date of 1460 BC. This phase saw the total eclipse of woodland species and the domination of the molluscan fauna by a species which normally favours broken ground and a dry habitat and is interpreted as representing the onset of agriculture and ploughing. It was followed by a thick aeolian deposit which contained an open country fauna.

THE PALISADE ENCLOSURE The discovery of a substantial palisade trench around the hill-top was unforeseen and has added a new dimension to our knowledge of the development of hill-top fortifications in the second millennium BC. It was recorded within and parallel to the main enclosure ditch, occupying the highest point of the spur. The trench was of variable width (normally 1–2 m), between 2.5 m to 3.0 m deep and enclosed an oval or egg-shaped area of some 11 acres (4.5 ha) 270 m from west to east and 245 m from north to south. The line of the trench is breached by two entrances in the north and east opposite entrance causeways across the main enclosure ditch. Of these entrances, only that in the east was fully investigated. They were extremely narrow and the gap between the flanking uprights at the east entrance could never have been more than 70 cm wide. The east entrance consisted of two ramped post-holes flanking a narrow gap in the trench. It was sited on the axis of the ridge leading into the enclosure from the east and the ramps for the post-holes were aligned outwards. The post-holes flanking the entrance were massive and had supported huge oak posts 1.6 m and 1.5 m respectively in diameter, which had been packed around with chalk rubble and which had been destroyed by fire. The north entrance was only recorded in plan but was clearly of similar type.

The normal profile of the palisade trench was straight-sided with a rounded base, the walls being frequently scarred with the marks of the antler picks with which it had been excavated nearly 4,000 years previously. Under suitable conditions, the 'ghosts' of the decayed upright posts could be recognized both in plan and section. The construction technique had been to ram puddled chalk around the bases of the uprights to provide some stabilization and then to pitch chalk

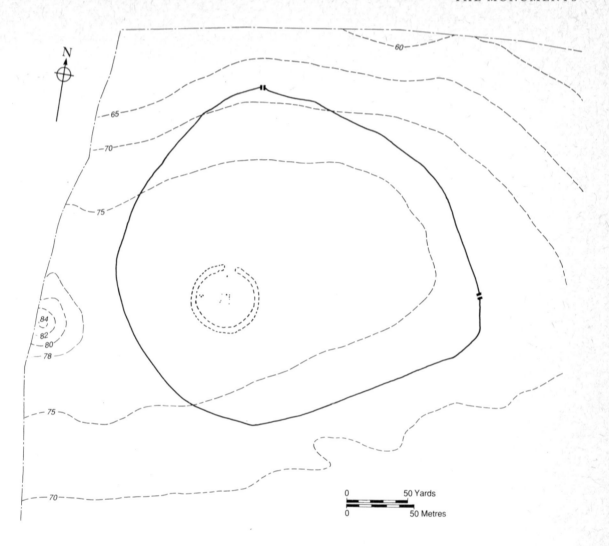

21   *The Mount Pleasant palisade enclosure.*

lumps around the posts, together with the occasional antler pick, up to
ground level. When excavated, the burnt or decayed posts were revealed
in plan and almost invariably, when all the upper packing had been
removed, the casts of the post butts were preserved in the hard puddled
chalk packing at the base of the palisade trench. As a result, it could be

ascertained that the foundation trench had supported timber uprights of oak set close together. The spacing of the posts worked out on average at two for every metre of trench. Therefore, in a palisade trench 800 m long, approximately 1,600 oak posts would have been required. In addition, the palisade as excavated was between 2.5 m and 3 m deep. To this must be added the unknown amount of chalk surface lost through erosion since the palisade was erected in c.1700 BC and to conclude that 3 m is only a minimal estimate. If one-third of the post-lengths were embedded in the ground (and this is a guess), then the stockade would have stood 6 m high above ground level composed of posts 9 m long. No evidence for internal supports for a wall-walk were found inside the line of the main stockade and if it was considered necessary to obtain an external view one must assume that a parapet walk was morticed to the stockade and reached by means of a ladder.

For the uprights of the stockade approximately 1,600 oak posts, each some 9 m long and a fairly uniform 40–50 cm in diameter, would have been required. To obtain such a large quantity of good quality timber approximately 900 acres (364 ha) of oak forest would have had to be exploited. In addition, a large labour force would have been required to select the trees, to fell them and to lop the branches, to drag them from the valley to the crest of the hill, and finally to erect them in the required positions, all this after a foundation trench 3 m deep, 1.2 m wide and 800 m long had been excavated into the solid chalk with antler picks. The motivation for the task must have been strong and contemporary society organized so as to allow the project to be undertaken amidst the imperatives of food production and exchange. Two radiocarbon dates relate to the construction of the palisade trench and suggest that this occurred around 1700 BC. These determinations are in good agreement with each other and with that of 1680 BC for the construction of the stone monument within the partially silted ditch of Site IV. The equivalent event in the sequence of silting in the main enclosure ditch at the north entrance is the formation of a friable ashy grey soil from which a number of stake-holes were cut and which is associated with the two crouched infant burials and a radiocarbon date of 1669 BC. It is at this point that sherds of Bronze Age fabric begin to appear alongside the Grooved Ware and Beaker sherds.

The artifacts associated with the palisade trench were obtained from the depression which had formed in its top after it fell into disuse. The material is therefore derived, but almost certainly contemporary with the period when the timber uprights were standing. The material

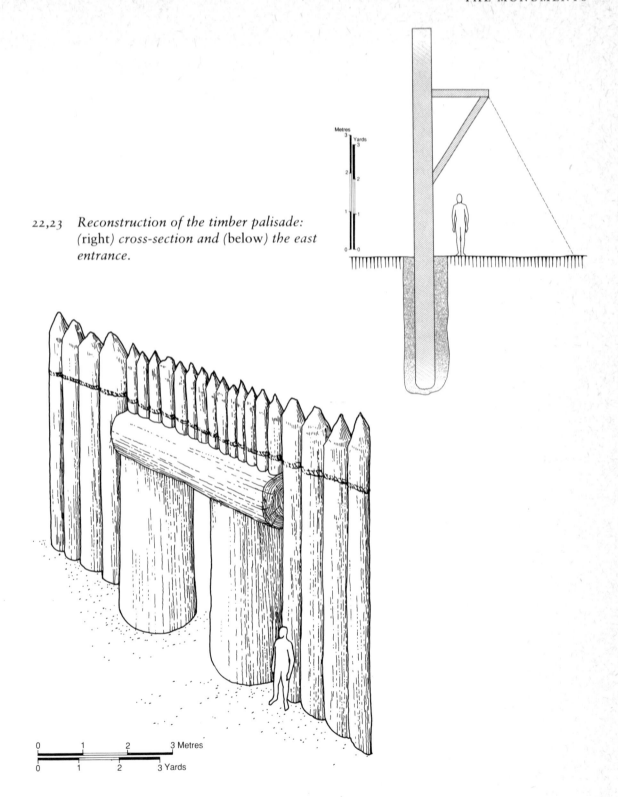

22,23   *Reconstruction of the timber palisade: (right) cross-section and (below) the east entrance.*

included flint artifacts such as arrowheads, a polished flint axe and two adzes, together with one complete and one fragmentary greenstone axe from Cornwall. Carved chalk objects were common and include 30 balls of possible phallic significance, carved blocks and a bowl fragment. Some 38 antler picks were recorded from packing around the timber uprights, but bone artifacts were restricted to one pin. The faunal remains include pig, cattle, sheep, dog, red deer, roe deer, fox and birds (song thrush, missel-thrush and pintail). Of the identifiable sherds the majority are of Beaker, although other ceramic traditions including Grooved Ware are represented.

The structure was ultimately destroyed at an unknown date by fire and dismantling. In some sectors the palisade was destroyed by a fire so fierce that the posts had smouldered and burnt throughout their length to the base of the trench and were excavated as columns of ash and burnt chalk. In other sectors, the posts had been deliberately dug out – presumably for re-use elsewhere, as seasoned oak posts 9 m long must have been valuable commodities. Other timber uprights had been left to decay in the ground, although the question as to whether they had been severed at ground level can hardly be resolved. The date of this demolition could not be established, but the probability is that it occurred within a century or two of its construction.

Mount Pleasant therefore differs from Durrington Walls and Marden in that there is good evidence for a sequence of structures over several centuries. The story begins with the pre-enclosure occupation which is represented by ceramic evidence only. Around 2000 BC or perhaps a century before, the large earthwork enclosure was built around the hill-top at about the same time as the Site IV timber structure was erected. The ceramic style in use at this time was Grooved Ware. The contemporary environment reflected by the molluscan fauna is one of woodland, when the hill-top was neither cultivated nor grazed. Around 1800 BC the west entrance to the main enclosure was narrowed by the extension of the ditch terminals. It may have been at this time that the Conquer Barrow was built on the enclosure bank near the west entrance. Indeed, the chalk rubble from the ditch terminal extensions may have contributed to its fabric. The episode, although of limited duration, is of significance in demonstrating a continued interest in the site.

The next major structural phase occurred about 1700 BC when the hill-top was surrounded by the great timber palisade and the Site IV structure replaced by the stone monument. The contemporary mollus-

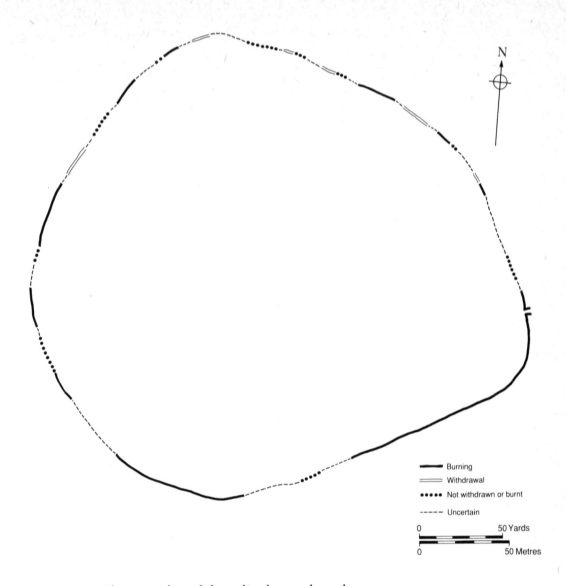

Burning
Withdrawal
•••• Not withdrawn or burnt
----- Uncertain

0   50 Yards

0   50 Metres

24   *Mount Pleasant: plan of the palisade trench to show
the methods of destruction.*

can fauna indicates that the woodland environment which had
previously prevailed was removed by a sudden and total clearance and
replaced by short-turfed grassland. The earlier earthwork, although
now three centuries old, had not been subjected to ploughing and would
therefore have been a prominent feature outside the palisade. It was
presumably for this reason that the north and east entrances through the
palisade were opposite causeways across the earlier ditch.

The palisade was eventually destroyed at some unknown date by fire and dismantling, but the evidence is that the hill-top was subsequently settled until the end of the second millennium BC. The molluscan fauna indicates tillage or massive over-grazing by sheep or cattle and that ploughing was continued in the first millennium BC is indicated by successive plough-wash deposits which contain pottery of Iron Age and Romano-British date. Various ditches and gullies cross the hill at this time, presumably with an agrarian purpose, but the presence of a single round-house within the confines of the old Site IV ditch, suggests the possibility of some settlement in the first century BC in addition to tillage. It was at this time that the stone setting and its outliers were broken up, presumably because they were an impediment to ploughing.

Mount Pleasant is sited slightly to the east of the modern county town of Dorchester which is itself based on the Roman city of *Durnovaria*, the presumed tribal capital of the Durotriges. It was also a focus of activity in the early prehistoric period, so that it sits between the monuments on the south Dorset Ridgeway and those on the chalk ridge to the north – of which Mount Pleasant is one. The basin within which Dorchester sits is dominated by such well-known monuments as Maiden Castle, Pound-bury, Maumbury Rings and Mount Pleasant, but recent excavations by the Trust for Wessex Archaeology in advance of new building in the town and the construction of the southern by-pass around it have revealed a greater complexity and richness of monuments as well as the less substantial settlements and industrial sites in which the monument builders lived and worked. This new work combined with that which had gone before has identified a grouping of Neolithic post-built structures that rivals complexes in the Upper Thames Valley, the Peak District or the Millfield Basin in the north.

Evidence for activity in the early third millennium BC comes from the South Winterbourne Valley and its adjacent high ground. The most important manifestation of this is the enclosure at Maiden Castle which is also the focus for a group of long barrows.

Late-third-millennium activity is well represented in the area. Field survey in advance of the Dorchester southern by-pass has identified two possible settlements characterized by high concentrations of oblique and transverse arrowheads and a general scatter of material indicating widespread activity. Maiden Castle at that time was extensively cultivated. A series of major monuments was constructed during this period which indicates intense activity in the area. The most famous is Mount Pleasant but contemporary with this was the recently discovered

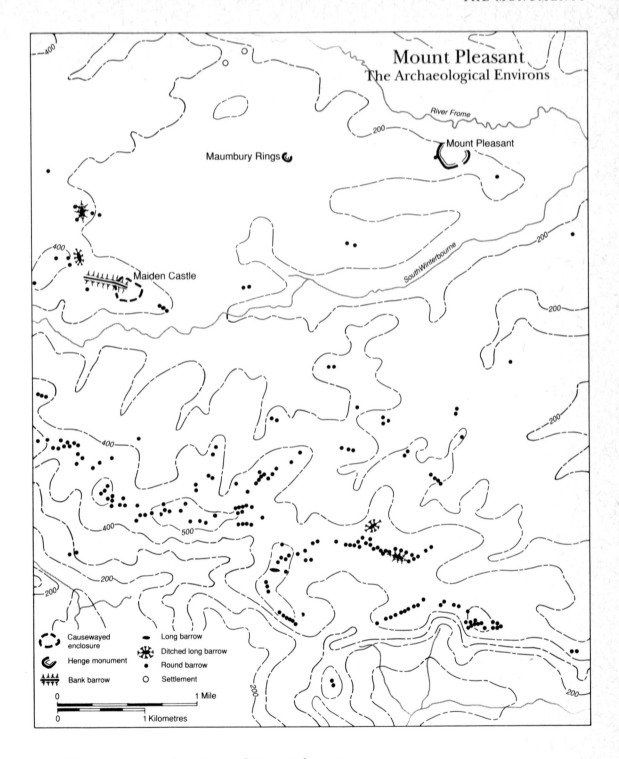

25   *The archaeological environs of Mount Pleasant.*

enclosure at Flagstones some 200 m to the west, a massive timber circle at Greyhound Yard in the centre of Dorchester, two pit-rings to the south on Conygeare Hill and a domestic site at Poundbury on the west side of Dorchester.

The enclosure at Flagstones is defined by a circular segmented ditch about 100 m in diameter which contained five burials. At four points distinct carvings were discovered on the sides of the ditch. They were of two types – linear scores and arcs or circles. The ditch produced a radiocarbon date of 2130 BC. At the centre of the enclosure were the remains of a round barrow with a central burial pit that contained a crouched inhumation.

The largest of the monuments to be discovered is the timber alignment at Greyhound Yard in the centre of Dorchester where a 50-m long stretch of twenty-one post-pits was uncovered. Each post was of oak, about 1 m in diameter and was placed in a pit 2.5 m deep with a large access ramp on the west side. This line of posts was also picked up in excavations nearby at Church Street. The alignment as exposed could conform to a projected circle of some 380 m in diameter. If the monument described a complete ring then some 600 mature oak trunks would have been required for its construction. Outside the post-ring a small demarcating ditch defined the site and may result from the construction of a chalk bank at the base of the posts. The radiocarbon dates suggest construction around 2100 BC and it appears that the posts were burnt above ground and the stumps left to decay whilst any earthwork was removed during cultivation in the Bronze Age.

These recent discoveries have established Dorchester and its environs as a major ritual centre from about 2000 BC until the onset of the Early Bronze Age and the environmental evidence based on soil micromorphological data and molluscan analyses from many sites indicates a primary woodland clearance in the early Neolithic around 3000 BC followed by secondary woodland regeneration and subsequent clearance in 2000 BC at the time of the construction of the monuments. This is a familiar pattern of clearance and regeneration which sets Mount Pleasant and its neighbouring and contemporary monuments at Flagstones, Maumbury Rings and Greyhound Yard at the end of a period of agrarian recession and at the beginning of a new phase of expansion.

1 Shaping the landscape   A ditch across the centre delimits the Neolithic causewayed enclosure within the Iron Age ramparts at Maiden Castle, Dorset.

Shaping the landscape

2 (*left*) The Neolithic West Kennet long barrow, Wiltshire.
3 (*left, below*) Hambledon Hill causewayed enclosure, Dorset. Recent excavations have shown that some of the fortified ramparts date back to the Neolithic.

4 (*right*) Aerial view of the flint mines at Grimes Graves, Norfolk, which were exploited by users of the pottery known as Grooved Ware.
5 (*below*) Recent excavations at Crickley Hill, Gloucestershire, have shown that this was a fortified promontory site in the Neolithic, with long-houses arranged along internal streets.

6 Top and side views of the three small chalk cylinders found on Folkton Wold, Yorkshire. Their curvilinear and geometric designs can be compared with Boyne Valley art (plates 8, 9), as well as with Grooved Ware decoration (*fig. 4*).

7 (*below*) The late Neolithic settlement of Skara Brae, Orkney.

8,9 (*opposite*) Decorated kerbstones 67 (*above*) and 1 (*below*; in front of the tomb entrance) at Newgrange in the Boyne Valley, Ireland.

10   (*above*) Enclosure ditches of a henge near Coupland, Northumberland, are revealed in this aerial photograph.
11   (*left*) The Winterbourne Stoke Crossroads Barrow Group.
12   (*below left*) Arbor Low henge, Derbyshire.

13   (*right, above*) Part of the silted up ditch and circle of standing stones at the great henge of Avebury, Wiltshire.
14   (*right, below*) Stonehenge, from which is derived the term 'henge', referring to circular structures enclosed by a bank and ditch.

Durrington Walls from the air

15 (*above left*) View from the north-east before excavation.
16 (*left*) Excavations at an early stage, seen from the south.
17 (*above right*) The enclosure ditch and Southern Circle, photographed from the east.
18 (*near right*) An early stage of the excavations, seen from the north-east, with Woodhenge in the background.
19 (*far right*) The enclosure ditch, Southern Circle and façade of the Northern Circle viewed from the north.

The Southern Circle at Durrington Walls

20 (*above*) Excavations in progress seen from the north.
21 (*right*) An early stage of excavation of the circle.
22 (*opposite, above*) Airview from the north, with the enclosure ditch and Southern Circle.
23 (*opposite*) Low level view of part of the circle before excavation of the main ring of post-holes.

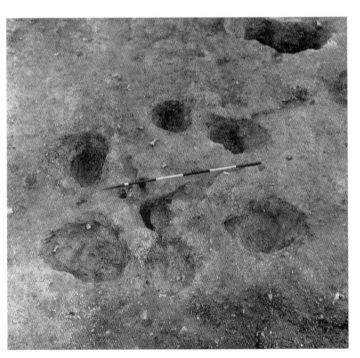

Post-holes of the Southern Circle

24 (*opposite, above*) Work in progress
on the circle.

25 (*opposite*) Post-holes and ramps of
the circle.

26 (*top left*) Ramped post-holes nos. 79
and 80 of phase 2 of the circle.

27 (*top right*) A ramped post-hole.

28 (*above left*) The inner post-hole ring
of the circle.

29 (*above right*) Post-holes of Phase 1
cut by post-hole 82 of Phase 2.

Durrington Walls: the enclosure ditch

30 (*above*) A section cut across the ditch.

31 (*left*) The south-east end of the excavated ditch.

32 (*right*) An early stage of the ditch excavation.

33 Airview of the circle from the south.

Woodhenge

Woodhenge is sited 60 m south of the Durrington Walls enclosure and was first considered to be a burial mound, until aerial observation by Squadron Leader Insall in 1925 revealed a series of concentric rings of dark spots in the wheat within the surrounding earthwork. The area within the ditch was totally excavated by Maude Cunnington between 1926 and 1928 and the name 'Woodhenge', as we have seen, given to the timber structure. The enclosing bank had been much eroded by the plough and occurred only in patches as a few inches of coarse rubble resting on a fossil soil on top of which were found great quantities of Grooved Ware. The bank was sited outside the ditch with external diameters of 85 m east-west and 88 m north-east–south-west and was crossed by a single causeway about 9 m wide facing north-east towards the Durrington Walls enclosure. Sherds of Grooved Ware were found in the primary chalk rubble of the ditch which was 1.8–2.1 m deep with a broad flat bottom 3.6–4.8 m wide.

The timber structure enclosed by the ditch comprised six concentric oval or egg-shaped rings of post-holes. In one important respect, therefore, Woodhenge closely resembles Phase 2 of the Southern Circle at Durrington in that both structures consist of six concentric rings of posts and were built to the same basic plan. However, the similarities end there, for Woodhenge is not only a larger monument overall, with a maximum diameter of 44 m as opposed to the 38.9 m of the Southern Circle, but the rings of the former are egg-shaped and not circular in plan. Furthermore, at Woodhenge the largest posts are not in the innermost ring, which may suggest that it was a different type of structure altogether. Finally, there is no formal entrance into the Woodhenge timber structure, as in the Southern Circle and the Sanctuary on Overton Hill, although there is a gap in the two outer rings of post-holes opposite the ditch causeway. One cannot be certain that no formal grave occurs within the Southern Circle as within Wood-henge, but there seems little doubt that the latter is not a purely sepulchral monument and that the burial within it is of a dedicatory nature. It comprised the crouched skeleton of a three-year-old child with a cleft skull in a small pit near the centre of the timber structure. In addition, the crouched skeleton of a young man was found in a grave dug into the floor of the ditch in its eastern sector and cremated human bones were found down one side of the upper part of one post-hole. This cremation had probably been placed at the foot of the post and slipped down as the latter decayed.

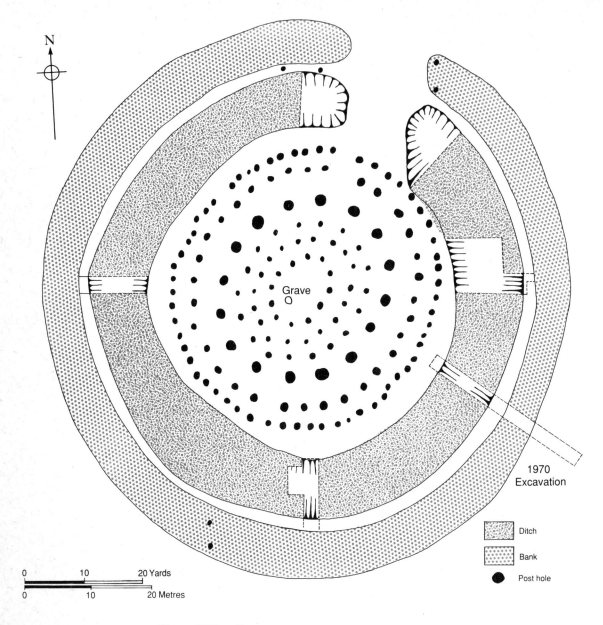

N

Grave
O

1970
Excavation

	Ditch
	Bank
●	Post hole

0   10   20 Yards
0   10   20 Metres

26 *Plan of Woodhenge.*

In minor structural details such as the provision of ramps and the charring of the butts of the posts, Woodhenge and the Southern Circle are very similar. The charcoals found at both sites were principally of oak and as at Durrington, only one fragment of a polished greenstone axe from Cornwall was recorded, although an axe of similar stone was recorded from the upper silts of the ditch near its entrance. This confirms that the dressing of the timbers was undertaken away from the site, but the importance of the axe is emphasized by the finding of two models in chalk in post-holes of the outer rings. In respect of material remains, Woodhenge and the Southern Circle are closely similar in that the former also produced a large quantity of Grooved Ware from the old land surface under the bank, from the post-holes of the rings and from the bottom of the ditch, together with a few scraps of Beaker pottery. The flint industry is also closely comparable, whilst antler picks, marine shells, lumps of sarsen stone and animal bones were also found.

Following the excavations at Durrington Walls in 1967, Woodhenge was of particular interest to those who were researching into the archaeology and environment of henge enclosures in southern England around 2000 BC. First, the relationship of Woodhenge to the comparable timber structure excavated at Durrington Walls was unknown, but could be clarified by radiocarbon dates. Secondly, it was clearly desirable to obtain soil samples for molluscan analyses from the fossil soil beneath the bank and from the ditch. This would provide information relating to the environment of the time which could be compared with that from Durrington Walls. Excavations were therefore carried out at Woodhenge in June 1970 by John Evans and the author with the aim of achieving these objectives by means of a single trench across the bank and ditch of the enclosure in its south-west sector.

The ditch was up to 5.1 m wide and 2.2 m deep with a flat base on which were found a pile of ten antler picks. A radiocarbon determination of 1867 BC was obtained from one of these picks. In addition, a small collection of animal bone from the primary chalk rubble silting of the ditch produced a radiocarbon determination of 1805 BC. The mollusca from the fossil soil beneath the enclosure bank indicate an early woodland environment followed by a forest clearance phase which can tentatively be ascribed to the middle of the third millennium BC and which is considered to be entirely a result of human activity. Finally, there was a period of dry grassland when the environment was free of wooded vegetation, and probably maintained as such by sheep grazing. The duration of this episode cannot be established, but it must have begun before 1800 BC when the enclosure bank was built. After the ditch had been dug it was left to silt up by natural means. The molluscan fauna indicates open conditions throughout its primary and secondary infilling with no question of scrub or even tall, dank grass ever having grown in the ditch bottom. This is in marked contrast to the situation at

Mount Pleasant and suggests that the environment was being kept artificially open – whether by grazing or land clearance is unknown.

The Sanctuary

Another timber structure of comparable type was also excavated by Mrs Cunnington in 1930 and is known as The Sanctuary. It is sited on a small level platform on Overton Hill in north Wiltshire and unlike Wood-henge, was re-built on several occasions, the final reconstruction being in stone. Unlike the Woodhenge, Durrington and Mount Pleasant structures, that at the Sanctuary was not surrounded by a bank and ditch, but like them it consists of six concentric rings of post-holes which are based on true circles as at Durrington and Mount Pleasant, and not on egg-shaped rings as at Woodhenge. The structural history of the monument so far as can be deduced from Mrs Cunnington's report are as follows:

Phase 1 A circle of post-holes 4.5 m in diameter with a central post-hole. This structure can be associated with the earliest pottery on the site and if so the structure is unlikely to have been built later than 2000 BC.

Phase 2 A larger, double ring of post-holes 11.5 m in diameter which followed closely on Phase 1.

Phase 3 The earlier rings were replaced by a circular post-hole structure 20.1 m in diameter with an entrance facing north-west. Pottery of Grooved Ware was found in post-holes of this phase.

Phase 4 An outer stone circle, 40.2 m in diameter, was constructed along with an inner stone circle on the line of the earlier post-ring. The outer circle was connected with the West Kennet Avenue leading to Avebury by two stones set radially on its circumference. The crouched burial of a young man was contemporary with one stone-hole and was associated with a Beaker vessel with 'barbed wire' ornament for which dates of around 1600 BC have been obtained on the continent.

In general, the timber structures of the Sanctuary resemble those of the Southern Circle at Durrington Walls and that at Mount Pleasant, in that they are circular, they are of more than one period and all are associated with Grooved Ware. However, the final timber structure at the Sanctuary was only 20 m in diameter compared with the 38.9 m of the Southern Circle, 38 m for Site IV at Mount Pleasant and the 44.1 × 39.6 m of Woodhenge. It was a much smaller structure and this seems to be reflected in the diameters of the timbers employed, as far as these can be established. In its final phase the stone ring at the Sanctuary enlarged the monument to 40.2 m – a comparable size to the others, but in its use of stone the Sanctuary should be compared with Mount Pleasant, Avebury – with which it is linked by the West Kennet Avenue – and Stonehenge.

Avebury and its region

The numerous monuments which make up the Avebury complex lie below the escarpment of the west side of the Marlborough Downs, within easy reach of overland routes such as the Ridgeway/Icknield Way, which extends eastwards as far as East Anglia. The major monuments are concentrated within a radius of about 5 km of Avebury itself. One of the earliest is the causewayed enclosure of Windmill Hill to the north-east dated to about 2500 BC and preceded by an even earlier settlement on top of the hill associated with tillage and dated to about 3000 BC. The causewayed enclosure itself is now defined by low, hardly visible, banks which enclose an area of 21 acres (8.5 ha) on top of the hill. It consists of three concentric rings of banks and ditches dug in segments and with plentiful human debris found in the filling of the ditches. This indicated that the crops grown were emmer wheat with a small proportion of hulled and naked barley and some flax. Crab apples and hazelnuts were plentiful. The bones of sheep, goats and pigs were found, but cattle were of far more importance and were slaughtered on the spot.

In the vicinity of the causewayed enclosure are a group of long-barrows, built as collective tombs to house the dead. They include both the stone-chambered kind as at West and East Kennet about 3 km to the south of Avebury, and long-barrows with no chambers of either stone or timber that were built as cenotaphs, or tribal markers, as at Beckhampton and South Street. In the ploughed fields, scatters of flint tools testify to settlement patterns that have never been methodically studied and which therefore we can glimpse only vaguely. Silbury Hill – the largest man-made mound in Europe, but whose function remains unknown, dominates the Kennet Valley and on the Ridgeway itself is the Sanctuary which was linked by the West Kennet Avenue to Avebury 3 km away.

The Avebury Circle itself covers an area of about 28.5 acres (11.5 ha) and has a median circumference of 1,353 m. The bank is between 22.9 m and 30.5 m wide at base and was once about 6.7 m high. Like Mount Pleasant, it has four opposed entrances, each about 15 m wide. Within the bank is a flat-bottomed ditch between 7 m and 10 m deep and 21 m wide at the top enclosing an area 347 m in diameter. Within the ditch stood the outer stone circle – the largest in Britain with a diameter of 331 m, and opposed entrances in the north-west and south-east. Inside the outer stone circle stand a pair of smaller, though still massive rings, each 103 m in diameter. No radiocarbon dates have been obtained from Avebury – the major excavations at the monument took place between 1908 and 1922. These were primarily concerned with excavating trenches across the bank and ditch, although the causeway at the south entrance was also examined in addition to the sites of some sarsens in the internal circles. However, Grooved Ware was found under the enclosure bank and can fairly be related to the earthwork phase. On analogy with Durrington Walls, Marden and Mount Pleasant, circular timber structures may be recorded in the interior in the future. The stone circles, Avenue and the Sanctuary stone circles are all part of a structural unit which probably dates from 1700–1600 BC on the basis of the pottery found with the stones. This would accord well with the stone phase at Mount Pleasant Site IV and the major phase of rebuilding at Stonehenge.

Stonehenge and its region

The nation has shabbily treated such a fine and important monument as Stonehenge. Successive governments have attempted to improve its condition and presentation to the public with limited success. Furthermore, our present understanding of the monument is based on interim results of unpublished work carried out in the mid 1950s and must be regarded as provisional until the definitive results of that work appear in print. Fortunately perhaps, it is no longer sufficient to study a single monument – even one as important as Stonehenge – as an entity in isolation from its surroundings. Each monument has to be seen as part of its evolving landscape and two field projects have greatly increased our understanding of Stonehenge and its environs in the past decade. The Royal Commission on Historical Monuments for England undertook a new review of the monuments in an area of about 13 square miles (33.6 sq km) around Stonehenge, where the landscape contains more prehistoric remains than any other area of the same size in Britain. Subsequently, and complementary to that survey, English Heritage commissioned the Trust for Wessex Archaeology to undertake an extensive analytical survey of the region for the purpose of formulating preservation and management strategies. This work, combined with the results of new environmental data from the monument obtained by John Evans, has enabled the famous site to be seen in relation to

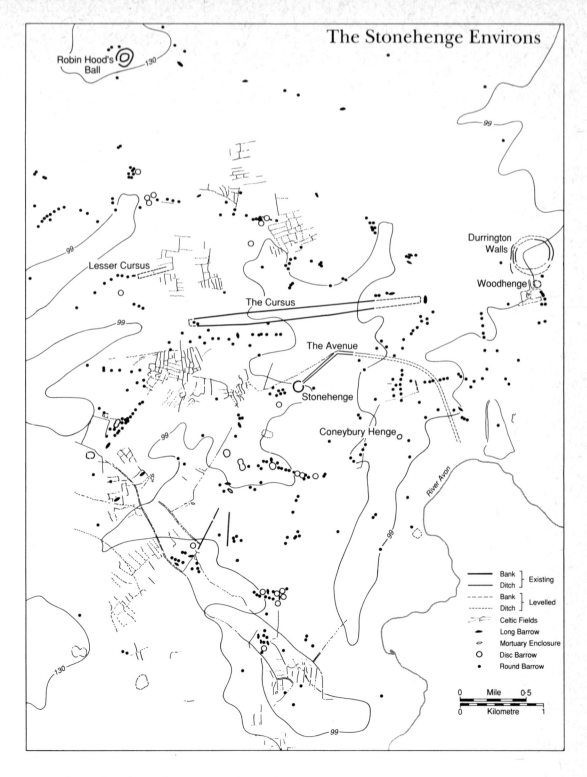

The Stonehenge Environs

Robin Hood's
Ball

Durrington
Walls

Woodhenge

Lesser Cursus

The Cursus

The Avenue

Stonehenge

Coneybury Henge

River Avon

▬▬ Bank	}	Existing
── Ditch		
- - - Bank	}	Levelled
········ Ditch		
⌇⌇ Celtic Fields		
▬ Long Barrow		
◠ Mortuary Enclosure		
○ Disc Barrow		
• Round Barrow		

0	Mile	0·5

0	Kilometre	1

27   *The archaeological environs of Stonehenge.*

environmental change and as an integral part of an evolving landscape as represented by the monuments around it. The timespan in radiocarbon years from the first man-made monuments to the latest burial mounds is from 3500 BC to 1200 BC – well over 2,000 years. The outcome of this work is that far from being a ritual landscape, devoid of inhabitants – as one might assume from the visible remains alone – the surveys have shown areas of intensive domestic and industrial activity contemporary with the major ceremonial centres. This activity can be divided into phases:

Phase 1 (c.2200 BC) An environment of woodland turning to open grassland under the influence of groups practising settled agriculture. They are associated with the causewayed enclosure at Robin Hood's Ball, long barrows, mortuary enclosures and cursus monuments and the structure of Stonehenge I. This last comprised a circular bank with external ditch 160 m in diameter, which is breached by a single entrance outside which stands the Heel Stone. Immediately inside the bank is a circle of 56 Aubrey Holes 76 m in diameter, which were filled in soon after they were dug and many of which incorporated human cremations. It seems probable that a timber structure existed in the centre of the enclosure in this phase, but the nature of this and of the Aubrey Holes must await publication of the evidence. Grooved Ware and antler have been obtained from the bottom of the ditch and radiocarbon dates from the latter suggest its construction around 2200 BC.

Phase 2 (c.1700 to 1600 BC) saw the abandonment of Stonehenge where the environmental evidence suggests an overgrown scrub-filled ditch. The shift in emphasis away from this early focus appears to have taken place late in the third millennium BC which also saw the emergence of Durrington Walls as an area of intensive ritually-based activity. This activity, which is associated with the large-scale use of Grooved Ware and large-scale engineering works in earth and timber, places Durrington Walls at the centre of the zone of intensive activity between the Avon Valley and the dry valley of Stonehenge Bottom. Surface collection of artifacts has defined areas of extensive activity and focal points for more intensive activity within that – including the exploitation of out-cropping flint seams in the Wilsford Down area. The area around Durrington Walls produced extensive traces of occupation at this time – pits, ditches, post-holes and surface scatters of Grooved Ware and stone tools.

Phase 3 (c.1500–1200 BC) The most dramatic aspect of this phase is the re-emphasis of Stonehenge itself, the development of the landscape

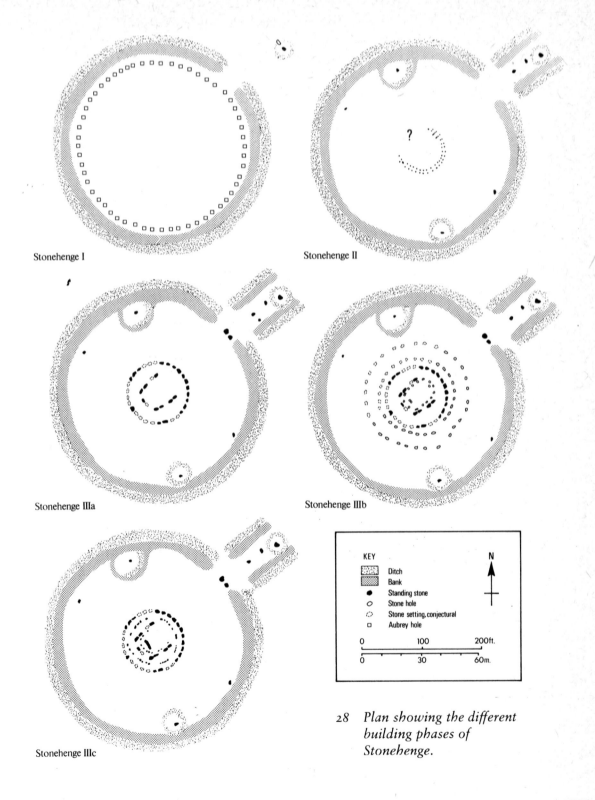

Stonehenge I

Stonehenge II

Stonehenge IIIa

Stonehenge IIIb

Stonehenge IIIc

KEY

Ditch
Bank
Standing stone
Stone hole
Stone setting, conjectural
Aubrey hole

N

0   100   200ft.

0   30   60m.

28   Plan showing the different
      building phases of
      Stonehenge.

around it and the decline of Durrington Walls and Woodhenge. Structural Phase 2 at Stonehenge saw the erection of a double, but incomplete, circle of 82 bluestones from north Pembrokeshire, the construction of the Avenue to the River Avon and Amesbury and the digging of the ditch around the Heel Stone. A radiocarbon date from a Beaker-age burial of 1765 BC indicates that the ditch had become practically infilled by that date when bluestone fragments first appear. Structural Phase 3 at Stonehenge is also part of this landscape phase. It saw the demolition of the bluestone circles and the transportation of some 80 sarsen blocks from the Marlborough Downs about 30 km to the north. The sarsens were erected as an outer circle about 30 m in diameter, with a continuous ring of lintels on top and a U-shaped setting within, consisting of five pairs of uprights, each with a lintel – the 'trilithons'. A radiocarbon determination of 1720 BC, from antler found at the base of the clean chalk filling of the ramp leading to Stonehole 56 of the Great Trilithon, is thought to date this phase. From this time onwards, Stonehenge and its succeeding structural phases – the latest date is 1240 BC – are surrounded by a development of major barrow cemeteries and the establishment of what appears to have been a largely ritual and funerary zone, unaccompanied by any surface indications of domestic or ritual activity.

CHAPTER FIVE

ENCLOSURES AND BUILDINGS DEDUCTION AND CONJECTURE

We have seen that by 2000 BC a new class of monument appears in southern Britain at the same time as the abrupt appearance of a fully fledged Grooved Ware ceramic tradition. These are massive earthwork enclosures with a circular bank, enclosing a ditch and approached by two or more entrances. There are just five of these in southern Britain, with diameters in excess of 300 m, at Durrington Walls, Marden, Avebury, Mount Pleasant and Knowlton. As a result of the excavation programme just described, three of these enclosures have produced the foundations of circular timber structures. They were not, however, the first such structures to have been discovered and excavated. The first such structure was Woodhenge. A subsequent interpretation of these remains by Stuart Piggott saw them as a roofed building of one period. In 1971 Chris Musson developed this interpretation and suggested that Woodhenge could represent two separate buildings, each with an outward sloping roof and central court. Subsequently, some debate has ensued as to whether these (and others) were free-standing settings of posts or whether they were roofed structures: the balance of opinion preferring the second interpretation.

The complex history of the Sanctuary was initially elucidated by Piggott and discussed in some detail by Musson in 1971. According to him, the initial building was a circular hut 4.5 m in diameter which was succeeded by successive buildings 11.5 m and 20 m in diameter respectively. The final timber building was eventually replaced by two concentric stone circles which were linked with the West Kennet Avenue and Avebury.

The Southern Circle at Durrington Walls was interpreted by Musson as having a central open court with a free-standing ring of timber uprights. The Northern Circle at Durrington was interpreted by him as a roofed building about 14.5 m in diameter, the four central posts perhaps supporting a raised lantern. This building was approached up an incline from the south by means of an irregular avenue of timber uprights through a façade of closely set posts.

The simple structure found at Marden was a single ring of post-holes, which can be interpreted as a simple circular building 10.5 m in diameter with a conical roof.

Finally, the excavations at Mount Pleasant recorded a circular timber structure (Site IV) which in its early phase was represented by five concentric rings of post-holes with an external diameter of 38 m. The very regular layout was designed around four corridors which divide the rings into arcs.

Any discussion of these timber structures must begin with a review of the evidence for the possible building forms that they represent. As the post-holes of the structures at Marden and Mount Pleasant had been heavily eroded by ploughing to the point where their bases had begun to disappear, they have no information to add to the architectural reconstructions of such buildings. The problem is whether or not the post-holes represent the remains of roofed buildings on the basis of the evidence from Durrington Walls, Woodhenge and the Sanctuary. Musson concluded that on strictly architectural grounds the structures

29   *Marden: reconstruction of the post circle.*

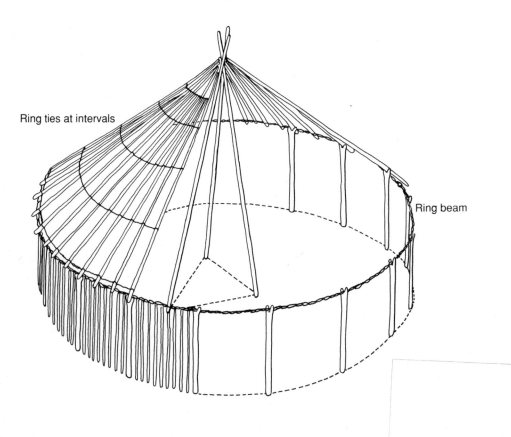

could have been roofed, although the evidence allows for other interpretations. It is clear that there can be no certainty about the intended function and form of the structures in question, in the absence of clear signs in the archaeological evidence itself. There are no other indications either positively in the form of preserved floor levels, or negatively in the shape of impossibly large rafter spans. Any reconstruction from the evidence of the post-holes alone must be based on a number of suppositions and inferences. These will include, amongst other things, the purpose or intention of the structure, its actual process of erection and possible sub-divisions into phases, and the nature and capacity of its structural elements, both individually and as a completed framework. The arguments therefore revolve around smaller questions of detail and interpretation, none of which is likely to be conclusive. Furthermore, there is little practical evidence to suggest the likely capacity and structural detailing of the buildings under review. The capacity of a building material, and especially of timber, is bound principally by experience and experiment, which may proceed at different speeds in different geographical or chronological settings. In this context, it must be said that work in the Somerset Levels over the past decade has indicated a degree of sophistication in woodland management and timber technology amongst early prehistoric communities, which would have placed the construction of such buildings well within the technical grasp of Wessex farmers in 2000 BC. Finally, there is rarely any archaeological evidence for the jointing and bracing methods used above ground and it is therefore difficult to make even informed guesses about the capacity of a structure in relation to the radial and lateral stresses imposed by pitched roofs and directional wind-loads.

With these reservations it is clear that, on the evidence of the surviving post-holes, Phase 1 of the Southern Circle was built of such light timbers that its interpretation as a fully roofed structure is doubtful, although it is not architecturally impossible. A more acceptable interpretation is that of a circular timber structure 23 m in diameter, with a narrow lean-to roof and an entrance nearly 6 m wide facing south-east. This roofed area surrounded an open central court occupied by a closely set circle of six posts, which was itself covered by a canopy or flanked by four free-standing posts, some of which had been preserved. The central setting of posts is only 2.2 m in diameter and has very shallow post-holes, so it was not a structural element supporting the roof as in that case the posts would have been nearly 9 m long, with basal diameters of around 15 cm. More probably, the ring represents a circle of free-standing timber uprights, or even the supports for a platform or table, as the focus for the structure, whether it was roofed or not. In view of the occurrence of a similar ring of smaller timber uprights at the centre of the Southern Circle, Phase 2, this interpretation is favoured. There is, however, no *a priori* evidence to confirm or deny such an interpretation and it must be considered in relation to alternative schemes.

Phase 2 of the Southern Circle must have followed soon after Phase 1, on account of the similarities of lay-out between the two structures. The patterns of the massive posts in the second phase are more complete and the potential rafter and beam spans quite acceptable in relation to them so that there is no doubt that the structure *could* have been roofed. In general, the post-pits and the timber uprights they supported increase in size and depth towards the centre, but the innermost ring has deeply set but relatively slender posts. The outer ring is broken by an entrance which faces south-east outside which was an irregular platform of chalk blocks and flint gravel on which a series of fires had been ignited. The only building form appropriate to this lay-out is an outward sloping roof with an outside wall and a high ridge surrounding an open central court. The inner ring of posts is best interpreted as a free-standing circle representing the focus of the building. Assuming a roof-pitch of 25 degrees (which is the minimum allowable), such a building would have had a height of about 10.5 m if there was an eaves height of about 3 m at the outer wall.

In his publication of a timber circle at Balfarg in Fife, Roger Mercer has made an important additional observation in respect of the Southern Circle at Durrington Walls. It is that the structure was set on a slope running to the south-east towards the river, and the drop in ground-level over the total diameter is of the order of 3.5 m. Mercer was able to point to a very consistent concentration of larger timbers within the south-east sector of the circle and has deduced from this that here we see a consistent pattern of levelling of the tops of timbers to produce a horizontal upper limit to the timber uprights as a whole. This is of the greatest interest, because a truly horizontal ring-beam would be required for the kind of roof postulated by Musson's study of architectural possibilities. However, a consistent but unverifiable problem in the interpretation of the structures is how deep it is necessary to bury a post for the purposes of stability. It is possible to make a theoretical calculation based on the lengths and angles of the ramps leading to the post-pits, and the assumption that the timber would pivot about the edge of the ramp and be positioned by gravity at an angle in

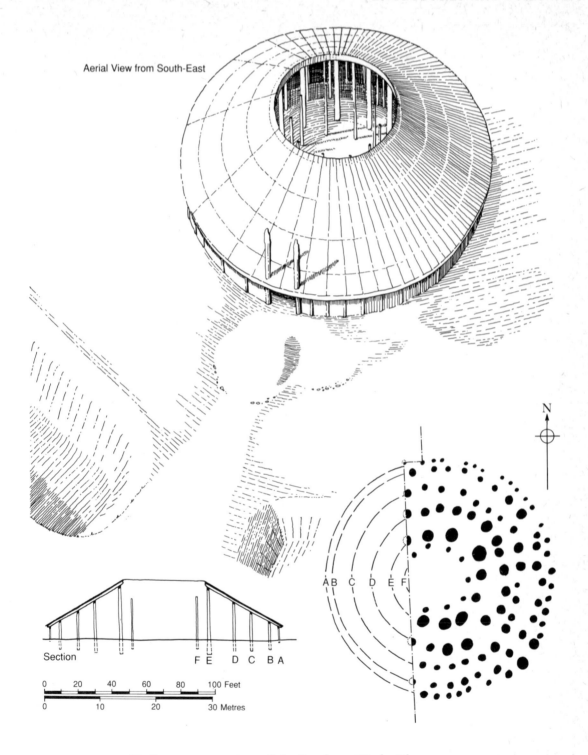

Aerial View from South-East

Section   F E   D C   B A

N

0   20   40   60   80   100 Feet

0   10   20   30 Metres

A B   C   D   E F

30 *Durrington Walls: reconstruction of the Southern Circle, Phase 2.*

the hole. This does not mean, of course, that it was always intended to bury one-third, or one-quarter of the post in the hole – a very wasteful process. Unfortunately, for earthfast posts it appears that there is no analytical solution. Accepted wisdom would have it, however, that a free-standing post would not be very stable unless the buried part was at least twice as long as the diameter. Proportion of length is not a very useful measure of structural stability, which is not necessarily improved by a high proportion of the post being embedded in the ground. The builders of the structures in 2000 BC would have had an interest in limiting the amount of below ground timber and hence minimizing the overall length of the post required. The roof-pitch therefore is entirely a matter for speculation save that a pitch of 25 degrees is an absolute minimum to enable the rain to run off. A roofed building hypothesis on this basis would give posts about 12 m long at the maximum height of the building, assuming 1.5 m below ground and an eaves height of about 3 m at the outer wall.

Some details of the projected roof structure can be deduced from the lay-out of the posts, others must remain entirely conjectural. Thus all but the innermost circle of posts must have supported continuous ring-beams or purlins, since the posts do not fall on radial lines and could not, therefore, have provided a direct bearing for the rafters. In a structure using such massive posts, it is slightly odd that there is little evidence for the use of long, relatively straight timbers in these beams. There are, indeed, a few cases where several post-holes seem to form a chord rather than the arc of a circle, but equally often the line is markedly irregular, suggesting that the ring-beam, if it existed, was probably made in short lengths, jointed at the head of each supporting column. Little more can be added about the roof structure as such; radial rafters, a metre or so apart, might have been crossed by smaller branches laid circumferentially as a basis for reed or straw thatching; alternatively, hurdle-work and turf laid directly on the rafters might have provided an underseal for a rather heavier thatched roof. In the absence of direct archaeological evidence, such details must remain purely hypothetical.

In the case of the Sanctuary on Overton Hill, Piggott produced a series of building forms which followed a reasonable pattern of growth and elaboration by dividing the various stone and timber circles into four separate phases. A detailed re-examination of these suggests that slightly different interpretations, either as roofed buildings, or as circles of free-standing posts, are equally possible. Taking first the interpretation of the structures as series of roofed buildings, Piggott's Phase 1

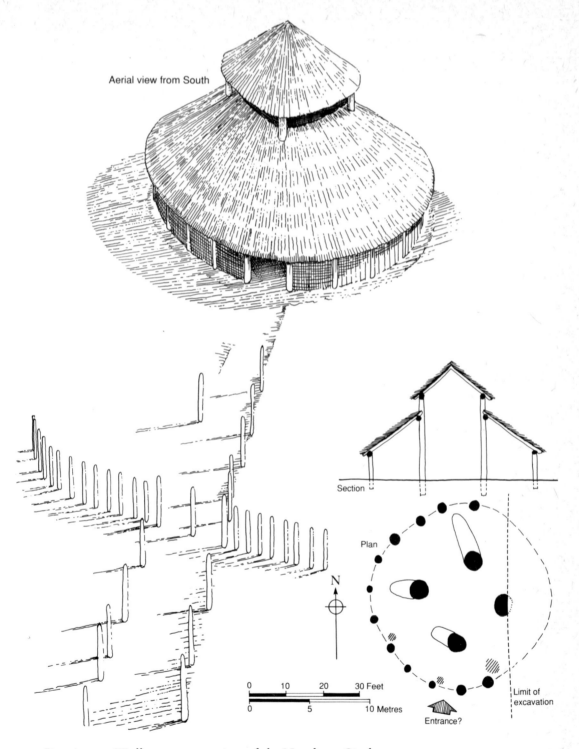

Aerial view from South

Section

Plan

N

Limit of
excavation

0   10   20   30 Feet

0   5   10 Metres

Entrance?

31 *Durrington Walls: reconstruction of the Northern Circle.*

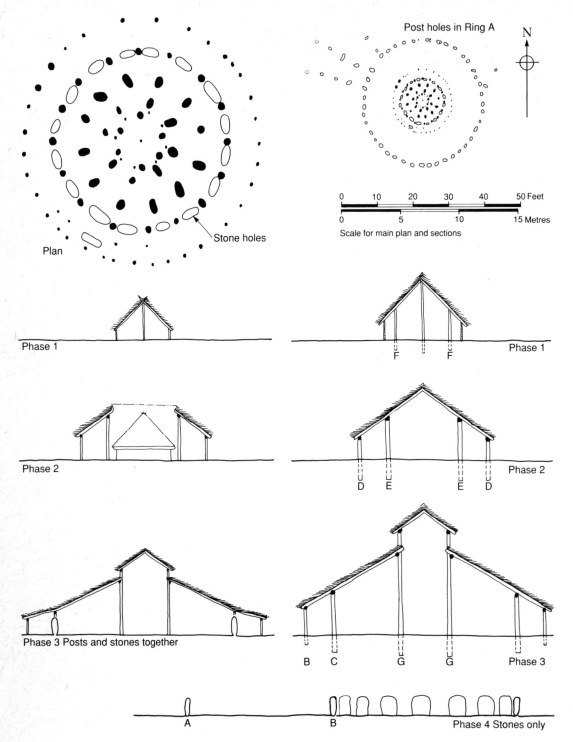

Plan

Stone holes

Post holes in Ring A

N

| 0 | 10 | 20 | 30 | 40 | 50 Feet |

| 0 | 5 | 10 | 15 Metres |

Scale for main plan and sections

Phase 1

Phase 1
F F

Phase 2

Phase 2
D E E D

Phase 3 Posts and stones together

Phase 3
B C G G

A

B Phase 4 Stones only

32 *Alternative reconstructions of the Sanctuary.*

'sacred hut' structure is unexceptional, save that the post-holes are surprisingly deep for so small a building.

Piggott's Phase 2 building used the 'double' post-holes of circles D and E, the inner post-cores of which in each case were taken as the later. On the whole, however, it seems more likely that the outer post-cores were the later, and that the replacements represent not repair during the continued life of the building, but a complete re-building *ab initio*. On this basis it looks very much as if a double-ring structure about 9.8 m in diameter (Phase 2A) was completely replaced in a single building operation by a slightly larger structure of identical design (Phase 2B), about 10.7 m in diameter. The close coincidence of the post-holes suggests that this re-building took place at a time when the positions of the original holes were still visible, either as the stumps of posts or as soil-marks in the ground. It is unlikely that the 'sacred hut' of Phase 1 was ever enclosed within the later building. No direct, or inferential, evidence can now be adduced to show whether the building was fully roofed or had a central court, but in the circumstances, and working within the framework of a roofed building hypothesis, it is probably simpler to assume a fully roofed conical design.

There is no necessity to follow Piggott in assuming that the stones and posts of circle C stood together at any time. The stones and posts together would have formed a fairly effective barrier to anyone seeking a dignified entry to the central area. It is equally possible that the present pattern resulted from a complete re-building in stone at a time when the stumps or soil-marks left by the Phase 3 posts still gave a clear guide for the erection between them of a new ring of standing stones, Phase 4. With this re-building can go the outer ring of stones, circle A, which may itself replace an earlier timber circle of which the only remains are four post-holes in its north sector. Phase 3 therefore appears to have been a triple-ringed structure of timber, replaced in Phase 4 by a double-ringed setting of standing stones which was quite clearly unroofed. If so, there is at least a suggestion that Phase 4 was a transformation of Phase 3 into a different and more permanent material, and that Phase 3 was therefore not a roofed building at all, but a simple arrangement of free-standing posts. The same inference could be extended backwards to cover Phases 2 and 1.

An explanation of the Sanctuary as a developing series of free-standing timber and stone circles has much to recommend it. In particular, there is no need to postulate a change in the *type* of monument between Phases 3 and 4, but simply a translation of the same basic idea into a more permanent building material. The great depth of the post-holes has already been mentioned. Both the outer posts and centre post of the Sanctuary in Phase 1 are considerably deeper than any found in domestic structures of similar age in the later prehistoric period. This greater depth in a sense supports the concept of free-standing timbers, since each post would have to stand individually, without the mutual support inherent in a walled and roofed structure. The extra depth is unlikely to have been necessitated by the inadequate cross-bracing of the roof. In the size and lay-out of its posts the proposed Phase 3 roofed building is considerably more economical than any of our later Iron Age houses. If it existed as a roofed structure, the rafters must have been efficiently braced by ties or other means; it is unlikely that the relatively slender columns of circle C could have provided sufficient lateral bracing through their own stiffness, however deeply embedded. This suggests a high degree of sophistication in structural timberwork, in contrast to the 'strength-by-bulk' appearance of Phase 2 of the Southern Circle at Durrington Walls.

Turning to Woodhenge, Piggott accepted that all the post-rings belonged to a single structure and saw the whole as a single building with a ridged roof and an open central court with drainage outwards and inwards on both slopes of the roof. On the other hand, the assumed unity of the rings is doubtful and other reconstructions in two or more phases become equally plausible. Musson therefore suggested that the post-rings at Woodhenge could represent two separate buildings, each with an outward sloping annular roof and with a central court. The post-holes of the initial and smaller phase (rings D, E and F) were built without ramps and might be compared with Phase 1 of the Southern Circle, whereas the second phase, incorporating the massive ramped post-holes of the outer three rings might be grouped with Phase 2. There is no stratigraphical evidence to establish which of the two possible interpretations is correct. However, a roof draining both outwards and inwards is not only unique, as no other comparable structures can take a similar roof form, but inconvenient, as an appreciable amount of rainwater would be drained into the central court.

The megalithic yard

In 1967 Alexander Thom published a survey of Woodhenge based on the concrete posts which were placed on the approximate sites of the post-

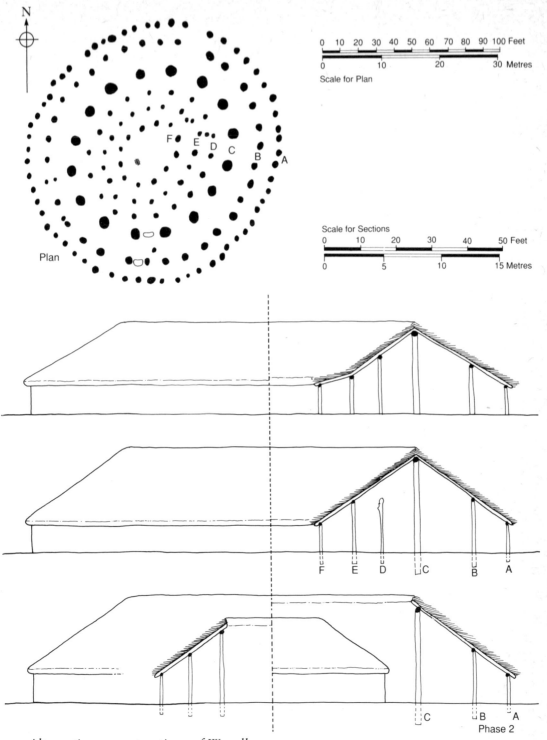

N

0 10 20 30 40 50 60 70 80 90 100 Feet
0   10   20   30 Metres
Scale for Plan

F E D C B A

Plan

Scale for Sections
0   10   20   30   40   50 Feet
0   5   10   15 Metres

F E D C B A

C B A

C B A
Phase 2

33   *Alternative reconstructions of Woodhenge.*

holes after the Cunnington excavation. He calculated that the structure consists of a series of egg-shaped rings with common centres for the arcs at the large and small ends. Thom listed ten sites with these egg-shaped rings which he divided into two types, both of which he claimed to be based on a pythagorean or near pythagorean triangle. In this, Thom was demonstrating his thesis that although most of the stone rings in Britain were laid out accurately as true circles, a large number could be shown to have been built around more complex geometrical constructions such as ellipses, egg-shapes and flattened circles – all of which had been set out in integral numbers of a unit, which he termed the 'megalithic yard' (2.72 ft). The implication was that in early prehistoric Britain there existed an advanced knowledge of geometry, including pythagorean right-angled triangles, and that the population was capable of skilled practical surveying in order to set out these large and sometimes complex designs on the ground with a high degree of accuracy.

The passage of some two decades has injected some healthy scepticism into these claims. Stone settings – circles and alignments – are unreliable data on which to base claims for such sophistication on account of their crude mass and tendency to selective disturbance. Unsafe assumptions were also adopted that all the elements visible on an unexcavated site need be contemporary and also that the present-day distribution of stones in the settings bears a significant relation to the original lay-out. Furthermore, the statistical evidence for the megalithic yard of 2.72 ft is not conclusive – although it is certainly interesting that the evidence points rather to a cruder unit with a striking resemblance to the human pace, normally accurate for survey work to within 2 or 3 percent.

So far as Woodhenge is concerned, there are considerable methodological difficulties involved in using the modern concrete blocks as true indicators of the previous positions of the timber uprights, as they were erected some time subsequent to the excavation after the holes had been backfilled. Furthermore, provided that the eye is not misled by Thom's superimposed guidelines, the lay-out can be seen to be very far from geometrically accurate. His theoretical ovals can be seen to miss many of the modern concrete markers by a metre or more and it is clear that the builders were not concerned to enshrine some arcane geometrical construction in their work.

Comparative structures

The structures from these five sites – Woodhenge, the Sanctuary, Durrington Walls, Marden and Mount Pleasant – represent the range of closely comparable timber structures (whether roofed or not) that were built in Wessex around 2000 BC. In addition, at Stonehenge Colonel Hawley excavated a number of post-holes in the central area, some of which may be ancient and some of recent date. Unfortunately, the evidence remains unpublished although Atkinson considers it probable that a timber building existed in the centre of the enclosure in its earliest phase.

A timber structure of rather different type was discovered from the air by Wing Commander Insall in 1929 at Arminghall in Norfolk. Excavations of the site by Grahame Clark revealed that two concentric ditches with a bank between them enclosed a circular area some 27 m in diameter, which was occupied by a pennanular setting of eight post-holes opening towards the single entrance in the inner ditch. Each post-hole was approached by a ramp from its south side and the two examples fully excavated were over 2 m deep. In both cases the posts had rotted *in situ* and the original diameters of the timbers could be established as 0.91 m and 1.06 m respectively. Both posts were of oak and when they decayed, weathering cones had formed in the upper parts of the post-holes, in the same way as in the Phase 2 post-holes of the Southern Circle at Durrington Walls. A radiocarbon date of 2490 BC was obtained for oak charcoal from the base of a post-hole.

Arminghall clearly represents a structure of different type to those at Woodhenge, the Sanctuary, Durrington Walls and Mount Pleasant. The timber structure could not have been roofed but may have been lintelled. Alternatively the posts may have been free-standing and carved with figures and symbols.

Other timber circles of broadly contemporary date, but of different type to those under discussion have been recorded in recent years. At Balfarg in Fife Roger Mercer has excavated an earthwork enclosure which surrounded a timber circle 25 m in diameter set concentrically to the enclosure ditch and associated with a substantial assemblage of Grooved Ware. In addition, there was some evidence for five other concentric timber circles within the free-standing outer ring, which appear to be palisade-type structures. A number of radiocarbon dates were obtained from charcoal in the main post-ring and ranged from 2465 BC to 2085 BC. The timber structures were succeeded by two concentric stone circles with a portal stone at the single entrance and the inhumed burial of a young adult at the centre.

A similar post-ring between 25 m and 27 m in diameter has been excavated by Gordon Barclay at Strathallan in Perthshire. Twenty-four large ramped post-holes were excavated and produced radiocarbon dates of 2090 BC and 2155 BC. The ring was enclosed by a ditch with an external bank covering an area 65 m in diameter and with two opposed entrances.

The single timber ring is paralleled at Moncrieffe in Perthshire and Milfield North in Northumberland though both are much smaller. We have seen that the Arminghall setting is horse-shoe shaped, as is the small setting at Croft Moraig in Perthshire, and a variation occurs in respect of the egg-shaped post circle excavated at Dorchester in Oxfordshire. The main axis of the plan of this structure was aligned along the centre of a cursus and timbers of the post-circle produced dates centering around 2000 BC. The circle was not surrounded by an earthwork and had been burnt *in situ*.

To summarize, therefore, a series of large circular structures was constructed in Wessex to closely comparable plans based on concentric rings of timber circles, at about the same time around 2000 BC and associated with the same very distinctive ceramic style. It is clear from the distribution of contemporary earthworks that these structures and the enclosures which are sometimes associated with them were focal points in the settlement patterns of the time. At the same time a variety of other timber rings were being constructed throughout Britain often associated with Grooved Ware, but of very different type from the clearly defined group of structures in mid-southern England.

Interpretation and function

The interpretation of those distinctive structures in southern England remains problematical. There are no particular architectural problems to roofing the structures and we shall shortly see that ethnographic parallels exist for such an interpretation. On the other hand, objective evidence is difficult to obtain and this has been sought in a re-examination of the abundant material remains which occurred in and around the structures at Durrington Walls. It has been known for some time that pottery vessels are represented by only a few sherds from the timber structures and by more reconstructable pots from the ditch, and that some variation is apparent in the Grooved Ware decorative motifs between the North and South circles – bearing in mind the small sample from the former. Furthermore, amongst the flint artifacts, transverse arrowheads and knives occur in greater proportions on the platform outside the Southern Circle as compared with scrapers, cores and flakes. What Colin Richards and Julian Thomas have shown in their re-examination of the material is that:

(i) Post-holes containing a large number of flint flakes contain little or no Grooved Ware.

(ii) A particular spatial patterning of other artifacts such as flint knives, arrowheads, bone pins and awls can be identified and is interpreted as evidence for formalized practices of deposition rather than utilitarian activity areas.

(iii) There is a marked fall-off in the quantity of Grooved Ware from the outer ring to the centre of the structure and a similar pattern was noted for flint artifacts.

These are trends in the depositional process that are not adequately solved by a purely utilitarian explanation.

The evidence of the fauna is even more striking. There is a general absence of butchery evidence from Durrington Walls and Mount Pleasant and minimal utilization of the bones beyond the removal of meat from them. Bones of pig are numerically superior across the site as a whole, whereas on the chalk and flint platform outside the entrance to the Southern Circle they are equalled by the numbers of cattle bones. Within the Southern Circle the faunal remains are dominated by the meat bones – humerus, tibia, vertebrae and radius – and the same is largely true of the primary ditch silts. In the midden outside the Southern Circle there is a peculiar predominance of the hind limbs of pig – all of which are very young. The material deposited at Durrington Walls therefore appears to imply non-utilitarian explanations in the case of pottery and flint and is of a special nature in the case of faunal remains, hinting at feasting and conspicuous consumption on a large scale.

Further evidence is provided by an irregular platform outside the entrance to the Southern Circle and by the midden found outside its north-east perimeter. The platform was composed of chalk lumps and flint nodules. An extensive area of burning occurred on it and the surface was littered with quantities of flints, sherds and animal bones. It appears to have been a focal point outside the structure proper where offerings were made and rituals performed prior to entering. Sited outside the north-east perimeter of the Southern Circle was a shallow oval hollow which was filled with a quantity of animal bones, sherds and stone tools, which has been interpreted as a midden. It is difficult to visualize the stake-settings around the northern and southern sectors of the midden as being contemporary with Phase 2 of the Southern Circle because their alignments intersect. However, there can be little doubt that the two structures are contemporary in part for sherds of the same pot occur in both. On account of the Beaker pottery found in the midden it seems unlikely that the radiocarbon date from it of 2320 BC refers to its terminal use. However, there are three unweathered sherds of plain earlier Neolithic bowls from the midden to which this date could refer. It is suggested that this mixture of ceramic styles and the siting and character of the deposit argues for the midden being a special repository for refuse from activities in its vicinity.

The nature of this association is of some interest and is clearly to do with the breaking of pottery vessels, the deposition of flint artifacts and the remains of meat joints – in this case a special selection had been made of the hind legs of young pigs. The origins of the practice of depositing collections of refuse in such a fashion as to suggest that they are the remains of ritual feasts or offerings can be traced back to the causewayed enclosures of the third millennium BC in Britain. The deliberate breaking of pottery vessels in and around stone circles is well documented. Similarly it is a commonly recognized phenomenon associated with burials under round barrows, represented by lenses of sherds, charcoal, bones and flints in the mounds of barrows which otherwise consist of clean soil thrown up from the ditch. The clearest evidence for the practice comes from the deliberate in-filling of the burial chambers and passage of the West Kennet Long Barrow near Avebury. This blocking material consisted of chalk rubble with seams of earth which contained sherds, flints, beads, bone tools and broken animal bones. This filling was a single act and a discussion of comparable occurrences in the British Isles led Piggott to suggest that the deliberate in-filling of chambered tombs was not an unusual phenomenon. The pottery assemblage was dominated by sherds of most types of vessel and were in the main, unweathered with freshly broken edges. This mixture of ceramic styles presented a problem of interpretation to the excavator for it was not possible to accept their contemporaneity. Piggott therefore suggested that the material consisted of a re-deposited series of ritual offerings, which had originally been made elsewhere in temporary storage places or an 'offering-house', where the sherds, flints and bones would accumulate until their fragments were included in the filling of the tomb. Piggott suggested an analogous situation at the

Sanctuary to explain the sherds, flints and animal bones from the stone and post-holes which he considered to be the remains of offerings and ritual meals.

The midden at Durrington Walls is likely to have been such a temporary storage place or 'offering-house' as was postulated by Piggott. The activities connected with the Southern Circle, involving the breakage of pots, the deposition of stone and bone tools and the consumption of meat, appears to have occurred principally on the platform outside the entrance to that structure and around its outer perimeter. The debris would then have been placed around the bases of the timber uprights and in the midden. Sherds of the same pottery vessel from the bases of different posts within the building as well as from the midden, testify to this process. The deposits in the midden would have been allowed to accumulate over a period which accounts for the range of ceramic styles found within it. It was from a deposit of this type, within the precincts of an enclosure devoted to communal practices, that one might expect some material to have been abstracted and incorporated in the blocking of a tomb like that of West Kennet. Clearly the radiocarbon date of 2320 BC does not apply to the later Neolithic material nor to the life of the Southern Circle. There are, however, a few unweathered sherds of earlier Neolithic bowls amongst the midden refuse and it is possible that these were introduced deliberately along with the charcoal which produced the radiocarbon date. In view of the special character of the midden this seems a likely solution and lends strength to the possibility that timber structures of the third millennium BC are to be found in the vicinity.

All the options for the architectural reconstructions of the Wessex multi-ring timber structures appear to preclude a purely domestic use for them. If one postulates concentric rings of free-standing uprights then a ritual content is clear. In the case of the roofed building hypothesis, which is favoured by the author, the most tenable interpretations in the case of the best preserved structures at Durrington Walls and Woodhenge, involve an open court in the centre of the building, and in the case of the Southern Circle this unroofed area was occupied by a free-standing ring of timber uprights. These architectural features would not occur in a purely domestic structure. Similarly, the smaller timber building at Durrington, though totally roofed, was approached by an avenue of timber uprights through a protective façade of closely set posts which again is not a feature that would occur in a domestic building. In the case of the Sanctuary on Overton Hill, the initial three phases were progressively larger timber buildings and there is no independent evidence to suggest that they were not domestic structures. However, like the timber structures at Mount Pleasant, the final building was replaced in Phase 4 by stone settings of a ritualistic character, which were linked to the Avebury enclosure by the West Kennet Avenue. This suggests that the earlier timber structures were also of a special character though not necessarily prototypes in timber of the later stone circles. Such lithicization of earlier timber structures is well attested not only from the Sanctuary and Mount Pleasant but also from Balfarg in Fife and Stonehenge. There are indications of a relatively narrow horizon for lithicization, between 1700 and 1600 BC on the limited radiocarbon evidence available, when earlier timber structures were transmuted into stone. In this connection one should also include Avebury where excavations may yet reveal timber structures pre-dating the stone settings. The transmutation of timber structures into stone is not a rare phenomenon in the third and second millennium BC. It has been invoked, for example, to explain relationships between megalithic tombs and earthen long barrows and has been demonstrated at several stone circles, as at Croft Moraig in Perthshire. Its relevance in the present context is that the process should indicate some special functions for the Wessex timber buildings, which made it necessary for their sitings to be permanently indicated by stone settings.

From this factual base and the conclusion that there were no architectural problems to roofing the rings it is possible to develop a little of the ethnographic evidence available. It is a truism that human relations are complex and that totally different structures can often serve the same function. Conversely similar buildings can often serve totally different functions, so that in one community an especially large house may be the private residence of an important individual, and in another a building used for public gatherings. The documented accounts of early travellers such as Hodgson, Hitchcock and Bartram in Georgia and Florida in North America in the eighteenth and nineteenth centuries shed light on the interpretive options which are available. Their accounts describe the council houses of settlements belonging to the Creek Confederacy in 1836. The naturalist William Bartram has left a graphic account of these Indians whose social organization is considered to be a paradigm for chiefdom societies in general. It has been estimated that the total population of the Cherokee, one of the largest tribes occupying an area several times that of Wessex, was of the order of 11,000 persons. At this time there were sixty 'towns', whose average population was less than 200. They lived mainly by agriculture supplemented by hunting and it is clear that the settlement was often very dispersed. At the centre of the larger 'towns' stood the circular council house. One such structure was the Irene Mound Site on a western bluff of the Savannah River in Georgia which was excavated between 1937 and 1940 and revealed the plan of a council house of the Creek Indians. The excavations conducted by the University of Georgia revealed a pattern of six concentric circles of palisade trenches and post-holes in the sandy subsoil, which represented the remains of a circular building 36.5 m in diameter, with a single entrance and a central hearth. A number of square or rectangular domestic houses were excavated in the same settlement.

It is known from eye-witness accounts by Bartram and others, that the council chamber was a large circular building used for various councils and ceremonies and was an important feature of the public places of the Creek Indians. Bartram described one such circular building:

The council or town-house is a large rotunda, capable of accommodating several hundred people . . . the Rotunda is constructed in the following manner, they first fix in the ground a circular range of posts or trunks of trees, about six feet high, at equal distances, which are notched at the top, to receive into them, from one to another, a range of beams or wall plates: within this is another circular order of very large or strong pillars, about twelve feet high, notched in like manner at the top, to receive another range of wall plates, and within this is yet another or third range of stronger and higher pillars, but fewer in number, and standing at a greater distance from each other; and lastly in the centre stands a very strong pillar, which forms the pinnacle of the building, and to which the rafters centre at the top; these rafters are strengthened and bound together by cross beams and laths, which sustain the roof or covering which is a layer of bark neatly placed, and tight enough to exclude the rain. . . Near the great pillar in the centre the fire is kindled for light, near which the musicians seat themselves, and round about this the performers exhibit their dances and other shows at public festivals.

Bartram also describes the use of the council houses for social and religious purposes. Immediately adjacent to the wall of the chamber at the Irene Mound site was a midden containing only large fragments of pottery vessels which were contemporary with the building. To the excavators this midden suggested some ceremonial, for Bartram reports that Cassine drinking was one of the chief activities carried out in the council chambers of the Creeks and since this drink is sacred it is possible that the vessels used were also sacred. The vessels from which the Cassine had been drunk were broken and sherds from them deliberately placed in the midden.

The remarkable similarities between the eye-witness accounts of the Creek council chambers and the timber structures of 2000 BC in southern England are very clear. It would, of course, be absurd to make too much of these fortuitous physical resemblances on account of disparities in cultural background, geography and time between the two groups. Nevertheless, the parallel is of value in providing a vivid reminder that such structures were built and used for communal purposes of a social and religious nature. More importantly the analogy provides an insight into the social purposes which lay behind such structures and their role in society.

Resources and labour

A factor which has contributed much to our understanding of the Southern Circle is its siting in the floor of the small dry valley which opens onto the River Avon. In this position it had been sealed by soil washed down from the sides of the valley and had not been subjected to ploughing or to the normal processes of erosion. As a result the post-holes and associated structures were so well preserved that the original dimensions of the former could be established with a fair degree of certainty. Furthermore, the timber uprights had decayed *in situ* so that in a majority of cases it was possible to establish the diameters of the posts which had been placed in the holes. By planning these post-'pipes' it was possible to establish the original ground plan of the timber uprights, and it was on the basis of this plan that Musson was able to reconstruct the possible building forms. In addition, however, it is possible to obtain information concerning the timbers themselves, the quantity of timber which would have been required and to make some estimate of the length of life of the building.

A number of posts had their butts charred to prevent decay before they were inserted into the post-holes. From the preponderance of charcoals of relatively large oaks in the post-holes it was concluded that oak was used for structural purposes. The diameters of these structural timbers can be estimated from the post-pipes and the length of timbers from the reconstructions provided by Musson, in which a roof-pitch of about 25 degrees has been assumed throughout. However Musson has emphasized that the angle of the roof may have been greater so that the estimates which follow are minumum quantities only. The amounts of timber estimated for rafters, ring-beams and trimmer-beams are inevitably very conjectural and these need not have been of oak. In addition, an unknown quantity of smaller timbers would have been required for cross-bracing and for the sub-structure of the thatch. On the basis that green oak weighs 67 lb (30.3 kg) per cu ft it can be calculated that over 260 tons of timber would have been required for phase 2 of the Southern Circle. The largest units in the structure were undoubtedly the entrance posts which weighed over 5 tons and 3.5 tons respectively. The weight of the larger post can be compared with that of the largest foreign stone at Stonehenge. This is the Altar Stone, transported from the Cosheston Beds in south Pembrokeshire, which when dressed weighs 6.25 tons and before dressing probably 7 tons. The problems of transporting logs, however large, would of course have been fewer than those of transporting large stones as they could float or be rolled. In excess of 1,036 m of timbers of varying diameters would have been required for the upright posts in the structure together with lengths totalling 1,524 m for purlins, ring-beams and rafters.

The selection, felling, trimming, preparation and transportation of such quantities of timber would have required advance planning, co-ordination and technical skill of a high order. Practical experiment has shown that flint axes can fell a large tree in under an hour and that a pine tree can be cut down in seven minutes. That the carpentry was of a sufficiently high standard can be assumed in a society where wood must have represented the major raw material for houses, utensils and tools and the use of the mortice and tenon joint, which must have been a vital component in the structures with which we are concerned, is confirmed by the recording of a beam with a morticed peg off the Essex coast, which was probably contemporary with the late Neolithic land surface. Chipped and polished axes of flint and stone would have been indispensable for the felling, trimming and preparation of the logs, but very few were found at Durrington Walls.

Two fragmentary axes of flint were recorded from the enclosure ditch and the old land surface under the bank respectively and one fragmentary axe of greenstone from the Southern Circle. In addition, a chopper was recorded from the ditch, two adzes from the old land surface under the enclosure bank and one adze from the surface of the platform outside the Southern Circle. The adzes are more likely to be carpentry tools than to have been involved in the initial hewing of the timbers. At Woodhenge one greenstone axe was recorded from the ditch and a chip of a second from a post-hole, in addition to the butt of a chipped flint axe and one adze. Few axes were recorded from the Sanctuary, Marden or Mount Pleasant. However, Woodhenge has produced two miniature axes of chalk, non-functional items which emphasize the importance such implements had in the tool complement and which make the absence of axes on the sites of these timber buildings even more noteworthy. Commonsense dictates that the hewing of the trees, the trimming of the branches and as much pre-treatment as possible would have been undertaken away from the building sites, so as to make the logs easier to transport, and it may be that the tools involved in this process would not have found their way to Durrington Walls, Woodhenge, the Sanctuary, Marden and Mount Pleasant. Nevertheless one feels that some carpentry would have been necessary on the building site, but that for reasons which are now obscure the implements involved in this work were then removed. This may have been so that they could be used again or they may have been collected for ceremonial disposal in a place which awaits discovery.

The source of such a large quantity of oak timbers is a problem which merits consideration, for as a result of human activity, the natural vegetation of the original ecosystem in many areas has quite disappeared with no opportunity to return. The total forested area in Wiltshire at the time of the Domesday survey in A D 1087 was 149,369 acres (60,448 ha), and of this, 29,040 acres (11,752 ha) were attributed to manorial woodlands around Amesbury which is now an all but tree-less region. Of the great forests which at one time covered a large part of the British Isles only fragments remain, and most of these have been very much modified, directly or indirectly by human activity.

The two native British species of oak *Quercus robur* and *Quercus petraea* are the most abundant of forest-forming British trees. *Quercus robur* is the dominant oak on moist clays and loams and on sandy, non-calcareous soil (e.g. Greensand) will bear a climax of vegetation of dry oakwood. Under favourable conditions the tree will make a long straight bole and may reach a height of over 30 m but a common height for mature well-grown oak in close canopy is 21–24 m. The chalk soil proper in the Durrington Walls region, however, is of the thin rendzina type where the natural 'climax' vegetation is beechwood and ash. To obtain suitable oak timbers for the structures at Durrington Walls it would have been necessary to exploit the soft alluvial soils of the river valleys (presumably the River Avon), or venture north into the Vale of Pewsey where the Greensand and alluvium would have provided a suitable environment for mixed oak forest. The exploitation of these areas would have provided a convenient method of transporting the logs, by floating them down the River Avon. It cannot be coincidental

34 Marden Aerial view of the excavations.

Marden: excavating the ditch

35 (*left*) The enclosure bank and ditch terminals.
36 (*below left*) Work in progress on the ditch terminal.
37 (*right*) Archaeologists methodically excavate the ditch terminal.
38 (*below right*) A section across the ditch.

Marden: the bank and contents of the ditch

39 (*left*) Section through the bank and the old land surface beneath it. Below that are much earlier periglacial deposits.

40 (*below left*) Waterlogged refuse near the base of the west ditch terminal.

41 (*below*) Antler picks on the floor of the ditch.

42 (*bottom*) Part of a human skeleton. The body had been included in the refuse thrown into the ditch terminals from the entrance causeway.

43 (*right*) The east bank terminal.

44 (*right, below*) The east bank terminal during excavation.

Overviews of the Mount Pleasant excavations

45 (*right*) Site IV from the air, clearly showing the five concentric post-hole rings of the circular structure.
46 (*below*) Airview of the excavations from the south.
47 (*opposite, above*) The post-holes of Site IV being watered in preparation for aerial photography.
48 (*opposite, below*) Site IV after rain to show the scars of modern ploughing.

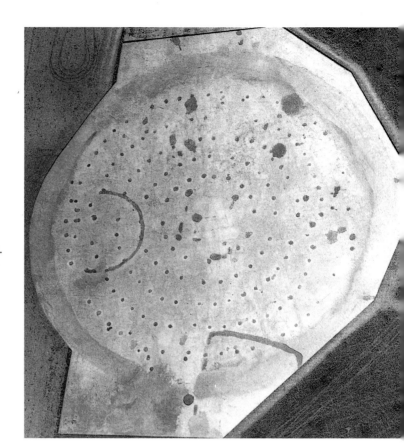

Mount Pleasant: the sarsen monoliths

49 (*left*) Fragments of destroyed sarsen monolith in a socket.
50 (*below*) The Site IV ditch to show burning, which equates with the destruction of the sarsen stone setting.

51 (above) Section of the Site
IV ditch to show the burnt
destruction layer.
52 (right) Stump of a sarsen
monolith in its socket.

**Mount Pleasant:
the enclosure ditch**

53   (*left*) A section across the ditch.
54   (*left, below*) The ditch under excavation.
55   (*right*) Skeleton of a child near the base of the ditch.
56   (*below*) Antler picks on the floor of the ditch.

57 (*right*) The palisade trench during excavation.
58 (*below*) Aerial view of the palisade excavations.
59 (*opposite*) Reconstructing the past: inserting a post into the palisade trench.
60 (*opposite, below left*) Charred butts of timber uprights in the palisade trench.
61 (*opposite, below right*) Impressions of butts of timber uprights in compacted chalk at the base of the palisade trench.

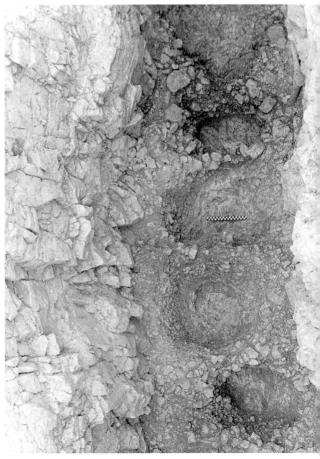

Woodhenge

62 (*left*) Air photograph taken in 1926 showing the Woodhenge enclosure and round barrows.

63 (*left, below*) Modern aerial view, with concrete stumps inserted to indicate the original timber uprights of the circle.

64 (*above left*) The 1926 excavations. The small mounds of earth capped with flints represent the approximate locations of post-holes excavated by Mrs Cunnington.

65 (*above right*) The 1970 excavations. Antler picks can be seen on the floor of the ditch.

66 (*right*) A section across the ditch – part of the 1970 excavations.

The Sanctuary

67 (*above*) The circular structure at the site known as the Sanctuary (right of the photograph), together with neighbouring round barrows.

68 (*left*) The Sanctuary's six concentric rings of post-holes are clearly visible in this airview.

that one flank of the Marden enclosure in the Vale of Pewsey is formed by the River Avon, or that 16 km further downstream the south-east entrance of the Durrington Walls enclosure opens onto a dry valley leading into that same river. The suitable logs must have been felled in this river valley or in the Vale of Pewsey, and in the case of Durrington, floated down the river and dragged up the valley. Two or three centuries later, this was probably the route followed by the Bluestones on their way from Pembrokeshire to Stonehenge. It appears likely that these stones were beached somewhere near Amesbury and then dragged along the route of the Avenue to the place of their erection. If so, they must have passed the south-east entrance of Durrington Walls which would still have been frequented. Clearly the route followed by the Bluestones was well prospected before it was used for that purpose, and the siting of both Marden and Durrington Walls may have been governed by the presence of the Avon, which played an important part in the transportation of the raw materials for the timber buildings.

In a naturally developed climax wood, the dominant trees compete with one another for light, soil and water. The weaker are killed or 'suppressed' so that in a mature wood only from 60–100 trees remain to the acre (150–250 to the hectare). One can relate these figures more exactly to the problems facing Neolithic man by employing Jessen's calculations in respect of the resources of oak timber required to build the great Viking houses at Trelleborg. Jessen has calculated that under natural conditions of temperate deciduous forest, oak trees with trunks 1.0–1.5 m in diameter occur at a rate of 7 to the hectare, and with trunks 0.5–0.75 m in diameter at 30 to the hectare. A calculation based on the average diameters of the timbers in Phase 2 of the Southern Circle, indicates that sufficient timber for this structure would be found in 8.75 acres (3.5 ha) of natural deciduous oak forest. These calculations refer to this one structure and similar figures must apply to the remainder of the Durrington Walls complex, to the Sanctuary, Marden and Mount Pleasant, so that the destruction of forest cover in southern Britain was clearly given considerable impetus at the beginning of the second millennium BC. During the Bronze Age, this process rapidly gathered momentum under the impact of the cultivation of crops and the grazing of sheep and cattle.

The length of the boles of *Quercus robur* in natural oak forest has been given as between 21–24 m and an oak trunk 20.4 m long without branching, was found near Ely in 1961, which has been given a radiocarbon determination of 2535 BC. That logs of such length were utilized in the first half of the second millennium BC is shown by reference to the dug-out canoes, which are invariably of oak, some of which have been published by Sir Cyril Fox. The range in the length of these craft is from 2.3 m to 14.7 m and an Irish example of 16.7 m in length is known from Lough Erne. A canoe 14 m long was found in Deeping Fen, Lincolnshire in 1839. The tree from which it was cut must have been straight-stemmed for at least 14 m and had a diameter of 1.8 m or more near the ground. It is now known that such canoes were used in the middle of the second millennium BC and it is clear that the provision of logs 12 m long and 1 m in diameter for building purposes would have presented no problems.

For building purposes *Quercus robur* is considered to be more durable than other types of oakwood. However, one should perhaps qualify this by stating that although the heartwood is very durable, the thin outer zone of sap-wood perishes rapidly. Field tests have been carried out by the Forest Products Research Laboratory to establish the natural durability of various timbers. These consist of inserting specimens of standard size in the ground and recording the time taken for them to decay. However, there are many variables to be taken into account, for the various causes of deterioration in timber are mechanical wear, decomposition by physical agencies, chemical decomposition, insect attack and fungal decay. Furthermore, conditions vary according to whether a timber is incorporated in a roofed building or whether it is standing in the open. In a building, the temperature is more constant, fluctuations in humidity are less violent and the movement of air around the timber is often restricted. However, any post which is partly embedded in the ground is liable to rot because it remains in a more or less permanently damp condition and the soil acts as a constant source of infection. Decay normally starts at or about ground level as the timbers are normally too dry to permit fungal growth above ground and too wet below ground. Decay is more rapid in light porous soils and it is claimed that chalky soils promote decay much more than do soils on gravel.

In effect, durability depends to a large extent on the environment of the particular locality in respect of climate, soil properties and the fungal flora. As a result, the resistance of the majority of timbers to fungal decay is not at all constant but varies considerably even between samples cut from the same log. Of the five grades of the durability classification established by the Forest Products Research Laboratory, varying from perishable to very durable, *Quercus robur* is described as 'durable', with

2×2 in (5×5 cm) stakes taking an average of 15–25 years to decay when in direct contact with the ground.

Investigations begun by the Forest Products Research Laboratory in 1951 indicate that, in contact with the ground, the life of timber is directly proportional to its diameter and not to its cross-sectional area. This indicates that the length of life of an oak post increases in direct proportion to the thickness of the wood. From the data given an oak heart-wood post 9 in (23 cm) in diameter should last for 100 years or more. However, in practice posts are likely to contain a proportion of perishable sap-wood and so their life will be shorter than this. As a rough estimate one can calculate that oak posts of large diameter, such as those used in the Southern Circle would have a life of about 15 years for each 2-in (5-cm) diameter of heart-wood. Oak posts of the Durrington diameters would decay at about this rate, as they would be preponderantly heartwood. However, as the timbers were incorporated in a roofed building and their bases would therefore be protected from the rain by the roof (this would also include the outer wall as the eaves are likely to have projected beyond this line), these figures are likely to be minimum estimates for the Southern Circle.

Bearing this reservation in mind and employing the factor of 15 years for every 2-in (5-cm) of post diameter, it can be calculated that Phase 1 of the Southern Circle will have had a minimum life of 60 years. Phase 2 of the Southern Circle with its five rings of structural posts is an altogether more robust structure. Once a building is established the components work together and if a post decays the load tends to be spread. In this way the building will stand until a key timber falls. On this basis, Phase 2 of the Southern Circle will have had a minimum life of 100 years, and more probably survived for the best part of 200 years. It will be recalled that these are minimum estimates based on calculations by the Forest Products Research Laboratory for timbers standing in the open. If one takes these factors into account it seems likely that this structure could have been in use for 200 years. It is of interest to note that the posts at the entrance to the building have potential survival values of 315 years and 270 years respectively. However, as they were not key structural posts this factor need not be relevant to the actual longevity of the building.

Finally, if the building survived for 200 years and was in use for that period, it is clear that pottery and flints could have been deposited within it at any time within these two centuries. If one considers the building to have been constructed around 1930 BC then the time-span during which debris could have been deposited is 1930–1730 BC. One might therefore expect to have several ceramic and lithic traditions represented within a building in use for so long, at a period when Beaker pottery was evolving in southern England.

It is possible to arrive at an estimate of the quantity of timber which would have been required for the Northern Circle and to make a calculation for the probable length of life of the building. Unlike the larger structure to the south, the charcoals were not sufficiently well preserved to enable any timber identifications to be made, but despite the erosion of the chalk surface that had taken place it was possible to obtain average post-diameters for the two rings. These data, together with Musson's reconstruction of the building, enabled the calculation that a total of 19.84 tons of oak timber would have been required for the Northern Circle, without including the façade and avenue. A total length of 99.6 m of timber would have been required for the uprights and 329 m of timber for the trimmer beams and rafters. In addition, a quantity of 2-in (5-cm) timbers would have been required for thatch. This compares with an estimated 260 tons of timber for the Southern Circle Phase 2 and a total length of 1039 m for the uprights of that structure. The key structural posts for the Northern Circle would have weighed an average of 2.27 tons each, as compared with 3.81 tons for the main structural posts of the Southern Circle Phase 2.

Employing similar calculations to those applied in the case of the Southern Circle, it can be estimated that the minimum length of life for the wall-posts is 105 years and for the centre posts 165 years. As the length of life of the structure is governed by the key structural posts, and decay could have been retarded to some extent by the roof of the building, these figures can be regarded as minimum values and the building was probably in use for at least the 165 years calculated on the basis of the centre posts.

It is the sheer size of the great earthwork enclosures, as well as the timber structures which they surround, and the implications for the mobilization of a large workforce in the region in 2000 BC which make the study of these earthworks of such interest. In the case of Durrington Walls it is possible to reconstruct an average profile of the enclosure earthworks as being an external bank 30 m wide and 3 m high which was separated by a platform or berm 20 m wide from a ditch which was 9.8 m wide and 5.4 m deep, with a flat base 6 m wide. This massive earthwork which enclosed 30 acres (12 ha) bears little relation to the eroded and barely visible remains on the ground today. In 2000 BC – or at any other time – it would have been a major engineering undertaking involving the

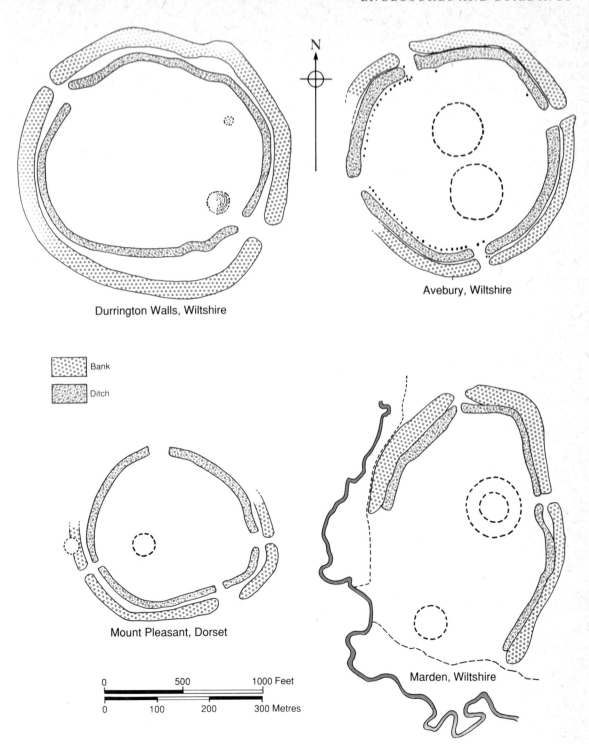

Bank

Ditch

Durrington Walls, Wiltshire

Avebury, Wiltshire

Mount Pleasant, Dorset

Marden, Wiltshire

0   500   1000 Feet

0   100   200   300 Metres

34   *Comparative plans of Late Neolithic enclosures in Wessex.*

157

excavation of 1,750,000 cubic feet (49,000 cubic metres) of chalk rubble with antler picks, baskets and ropes – bearing in mind that the weight per cubic foot of moist chalk is 1 cwt (50 kg); the removal of the rubble from the ditch; the transportation of this material across the berm which could be as wide as 42 m but was never less than 6 m and the dumping of the baskets of chalk on the bank, which was usually uphill from the ditch and which, when near completion, would have been about 3 m high.

Richard Atkinson evolved an empirical formula for calculating the human effort involved in these undertakings and calculated that an estimated 900,000 man-hours would have been involved.

There are a number of unverifiable estimates and approximations involved in such calculations and using data published on human capacity for digging earthworks before the advent of mechanical excavators and not an empirical formula, Bill Startin has arrived at a figure of 500,000 man-hours for building the same earthwork and a probable workforce of between 250 and 500.

It is instructive to compare these calculations for the Durrington bank and ditch and the logistics necessary for its construction with those obtained for the Avebury earthwork. The internal diameter of the Avebury ditch is 347 m and sections of it excavated by Sir George Gray between 1908 and 1922 show that as excavated it is some 21.3 m wide with a flat bottom 2.4–5.1 m wide which is between 7 m and 10 m below the present surface. The bank has a diameter of 426 m and is from 22.8–30.4 m wide whilst still standing 4.2–5.4 m above ground level. A berm 3.6 m wide was present in the south-east sector, whereas a narrower berm, or none at all was present elsewhere. Atkinson has suggested that 1,500,000 man-hours were required for the construction of the earthwork using the same empirical formula as for Durrington Walls. Using data published before the advent of mechanical aids, Startin has arrived at a figure of 500,000 man-hours – the same as for Durrington Walls.

These great engineering works must have taken place within a carefully designed logistical framework. The main digging implement was the pick made from red deer antler, which is a resilient material and particularly well shaped for the purpose. The picks would have become worn after a short time and so would need to be replaced, sometimes almost daily. At Durrington Walls a pile of fifty-seven antler picks was found in the enclosure ditch terminal. Juliet Clutton-Brock has undertaken a fresh study of these picks from Durrington Walls along with those from the flint mines of Grime's Graves in Norfolk which

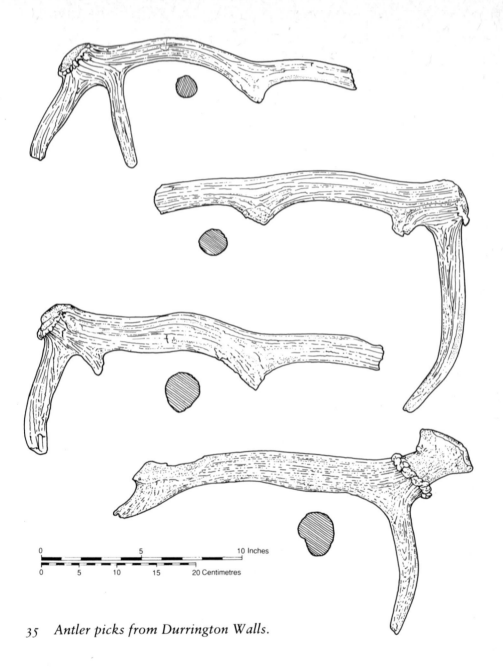

35   Antler picks from Durrington Walls.

throws an interesting light on the arrangements that would have been necessary to ensure a plentiful supply of these essential implements.

The preferred habitat of the red deer is fairly dense woodland and their most important food is browse. They do not primarily graze on grass and to produce antlers of the size and fine condition found at Durrington Walls the deer must have been living in optimum conditions. Only a small proportion of the antler picks from Durrington had been gnawed and deer only chew their own antlers after they are cast in areas where the browse is inadequate. It is probable that in a mature deciduous forest where a population of deer was in balance with the ecosystem it would be reasonable to suggest a distribution of one red deer to 10 hectares. Each stag will produce up to 18 pairs of antlers in its lifetime and at Durrington there were almost equal numbers of right and left antlers so that all available material was used. Clutton-Brock therefore suggests that antler was such a vital raw material that red deer were not hunted for food but were conserved and managed so that each year they would supply a plentiful crop of fresh antlers within walking distance of human settlement. Of the antlers from Durrington Walls, 290 were cast and 42 were from dead animals. Vast quantities of antlers would have been required for these engineering works in 2000 BC and it seems unlikely that local supplies would have been enough. As an important commodity they could have been derived from a variety of sources via the trade networks which had already been opened up for other materials. Antler must therefore be seen as one of the most valuable resources in prehistoric economies, the collection and distribution of which was an important element in the economic fabric of the time.

Timber was clearly an important raw material. It has been estimated that 264 tons of structural oak timber would have been required for the Southern Circle at Durrington Walls. The exploitation of that much timber at considerable distances from the construction sites represented a major expenditure of energy and human resources. In the forests the trees would have been selected, felled, trimmed, de-barked, cut to predetermined lengths and then conveyed to the construction sites. While such timber procurement would have undoubtedly affected the tree communities of the area, the overall impact of the activities was probably less severe than the wholesale destruction sometimes postulated. Because trees would have been used which represented only a total range of sizes available, from an ecological standpoint this would have been analogous to the thinning practised by modern foresters.

Communities may have provided timber as part of their contribution. Rivers would have facilitated the transportation of logs to the construction sites and the Wessex centres are sited near rivers. The scarcity of stone axes at construction sites indicates that material evidence of prehistoric logging is to be found in the surrounding landscape. A great amount of lithic material has come from the region including polished axes and fragments, evidence for the manufacture of those implements, choppers, rough hammers and the heavy duty implements necessary for woodland management. The timber industry is another measure of the magnitude and complexity of the socio-economic system in southern Britain around 2000 BC.

There is a big difference between the labour requirements for the public works that were built between 3000 BC and 2500 BC – causewayed enclosures, chambered tombs and the like – and the major public undertakings of 2000 BC. They are separated by about 500 years and in that period there is some evidence to suggest an economic recession and forest regeneration. The economic cycle is one of discontinuous growth not of steady development. The additional labour requirements imply a higher population and a greater mobilization of the workforce. Ethnographic parallels suggest a population density of very roughly 10 per square kilometre. On that basis Wessex would have had a population of about 50,000 in 2000 BC of which between 1 per cent and 5 per cent could have undertaken the building of Durrington Walls, Marden, Avebury, Mount Pleasant and Knowlton. Monument building in Wessex need not therefore have made a crushing demand on resources unless the workforce was drawn from a restricted area. If these estimates are of the right order the work would hardly have interfered with the essential business of food production, even allowing for the need to produce a surplus whilst building was in progress.

CHAPTER SIX

CEREMONY AND SOCIETY

The discovery of the large enclosures and the timber buildings that were associated with them raises the important question as to why some societies build monuments that can consume a large amount of labour and yet apparently have no practical function. What meaning did such monuments have for societies in Wessex in 2000 BC and what can they tell us about the nature of society at that time? The background within which the answers to these questions may be found is in the economic cycle of the third millennium BC about which it is now possible to make some general deductions.

It has become apparent that 1,000 years after the arrival of the first farmers on Salisbury Plain an economic crisis had developed. The population was growing; it has been calculated that the descendants of a family of 10 people – 5 men, 4 women and 1 child – could have suffered more than 1,700 deaths in 300 years and still have expanded to a community of over 500 people. Burl has therefore made a calculation based on 80 families at the beginning of the Neolithic period on Salisbury Plain which shows a hypothetical but feasible increase from nearly 1,000 people to 7,000 people over 1,000 years – over seven times the number of the first settlers. As a result there were more people to feed, more crops were grown, more stock were bred, more land was brought into cultivation and the soils were over-exploited. Competitive farmland must have increased and this is reflected in the evidence from the sites of the time. The timber palisade surrounding Hambledon Hill in Dorset was burnt down. In its ashes was the skeleton of a young man with a flint arrowhead in his chest. He appears to have been carrying a child when he was hit – possibly in an attempt to save it from the fire. At Carn Brae in Cornwall the hill-top was surrounded by a rampart of huge stones – some weighing over two tons. More than 700 arrowheads lay around this rampart, many of them around the gateway. At Crickley Hill in Gloucestershire a rectangular house was set on fire and more than 200 arrowheads were found in its ashes. Many examples of individual killings may also be quoted – from Stonehenge itself, the West Kennet Long Barrow and the Fengate mortuary enclosure in the East Anglian

Fens. In such a period of competition and land hunger therefore, conflicts occur, territories are formed and leaders emerge.

By 2500 BC, therefore, large areas of land in Wessex were exhausted through over-exploitation. This took the form of de-forestation to clear fields and to provide timber for dwellings and fuel; over-intensive arable cultivation which reduced the original thick brown-earths to the thin rendzinas that we see today, and through de-turfing for houses. It has been calculated, for instance, that the needs of one turf-walled building – not particularly large and resembling that recorded at Honington in Suffolk – would have required one acre of turf. A village of twenty buildings would have devastated the surrounding pasture.

The mid-third millennium BC must therefore be seen as a time of economic recession and retraction in the landscape. However, the two centuries before 2000 BC show a renewal of clearance and the establishment of a subsistence strategy which was more efficient in comparison with the extensive and wasteful land-use strategies employed in earlier centuries. Light ploughs were used and marks of their traction have been recorded at a number of sites including South Street, Wiltshire and Simondston in Glamorgan. Arable cultivation was again widespread, grain has been recorded from pits on many settlements, some associated with Grooved Ware as at Barton Court Farm in Oxfordshire, and stock raising was also important. By 2000 BC subsistence methods had evolved to the point where the problems posed by secondary environments had been mastered and a second phase of expansion was under way. On the Nene river terrace at Fengate, we have seen that stockmen laid out a network of ditches – probably crowned originally with hedges and banks – to control cattle. Similar field systems can be located along the Fen edge for at least 32 km. Ostensibly, however, this success was first achieved in the upper reaches of the chalkland river systems of Wiltshire and Dorset and the construction of the public monuments – timber buildings and earthwork enclosures – may be seen as a response to this.

We have seen that extensive evidence is available for regional developments in later Neolithic Britain and that a number of core areas can be defined which include Wessex, the Upper Thames Valley, the Peak District, the Orkney Islands and the Boyne Valley. Of these, Wessex is notable in terms of its early development of regional groups based around the building of causewayed enclosures, burial in non-megalithic long barrows and the later megalithic barrows and tombs. The combination of these monuments with the development of ritual landscapes, and the construction of massive ceremonial monuments such as bank barrows and cursus, provide a secure basis for postulating long-term control of the area by a few individuals. The natural advantages which made the area so important are that the soils of Wessex make rich agricultural land, there are good sources of flint in the region and it provides a natural convergence of routes along which axes, pottery and other goods were moved. Powerful individuals in Wessex were therefore able to control local agricultural production and the manufacture of implements made from the local flint. Because of its location they were also able to control the distribution of other goods from outside the region, thus enhancing the importance of Wessex by comparison with nearby regions. The development of the large communal monuments must have been conspicuous instruments in both gaining and controlling that power.

Following the economic recession in Wessex, at about 2000 BC there was an intensification of monument building and also an increase in the size of monuments as well as the adoption of a new style of pottery. It is also possible to identify the re-emergence of five territorial groups within the Wessex region. That at Knowlton in Dorset at the south-east edge of Cranborne Chase was well placed to exploit the interaction between the chalklands of the Chase and the Tertiary basin beyond. Avebury, Durrington Walls and Mount Pleasant were arguably the three premier centres of Wessex at that time. Avebury would have served communities from the Kennet Valley system and the three clay vales fringing the north Wessex downs; Durrington Walls the Avon system commanding Salisbury Plain and the Vales of Warminster and Wardour; Mount Pleasant the coastal zone chalklands and the Tertiary basin of south Dorset. The monuments and the territories which they served illustrate the re-emergence after some 500 years of a new, outward-looking and expansive social order.

The building of communal monuments – the great henges and timber buildings was a deliberate strategy by those holding power to maintain that social order and to increase their control over it. They were symbols of group identity which not only assisted in the cohesion of the group but would also have contributed to increased status and power for the individual who could manipulate the feelings of power and permanence which they must have inspired in the population. John Cherry has considered the role of such monuments in early societies and has pointed out that their construction consistently occurs at two points in the cyclical development of such groups. The first period of monument building takes place while societies are at a formative stage and assists in binding them into a coherent organization by providing a common focus for their activities and aspirations. There may then be a reduction in the intensity of public works until a second phase of monument building takes place as the fabric of that society decays. At this stage their construction can act as a way of focusing the communal will and effort as an act of integration. Viewed in retrospect across 5,000 years of human settlement in these islands, public monuments coincide with periods of change. In Wessex, the henge monuments and timber buildings involved a far greater investment of manpower than earlier monuments and they belong to a formative stage when a phase of economic expansion was under way.

Questions about the use of the great enclosures has, up to now, polarized between views as to whether they were symbols of group identity manipulated by powerful individuals to enchance their own status, or whether they were the centres of learned orders, skilled in advanced astronomical and geometrical knowledge. The protagonist of the latter theory has been Euan MacKie who claimed the existence of a central authority with astronomical and magical expertise and saw the timber buildings as the residences of this élite group. This theory was largely based on the work of Alexander Thom who espoused the view that some very advanced astronomical and geometrical knowledge had been accumulated in Brittany and Britain well before 1800 BC. From this, MacKie went on to postulate a learned and skilled professional order of wise men whose members were able to pursue their studies full-time while supported by the population, and could command the labour required to erect the hundreds of henge monuments, stone circles and standing stones, some of which were their 'observatories'.

The timber buildings therefore provided crucially important direct evidence for a specialist class of astronomer priests which is required by Thom's theories. For MacKie, these buildings were the residences, temples and training schools of the learned orders which undertook the centuries of work which would have been necessary at the 'observatories'. These specialists would have been supported by tributes of food and labour by the peasant population and MacKie saw the rubbish debris within the buildings as simple domestic rubbish and not ritual in character. In this, he has been followed by Aubrey Burl who interprets Durrington Walls as having a permanent population of non-farming specialists who lived off a surplus of food provided by the surrounding peasant populations.

Recent work has, however, cast doubt on the propositions argued by Professor Thom some fifteen years ago, primarily in his misunderstanding of archaeological data and imprecision in the demonstration of astronomical alignments. For the archaeologist prepared to be convinced of the possession of advanced astronomical knowledge in 2000 BC the claims are now threadbare and the evidence for them is contentious. Thom's conclusions, if correct, pointed to Britain as the focus of a scientifically learned society whose mathematical, geometrical and astronomical discoveries anticipated those of the Babylonians and Greeks. The unreliability of the data – the stone circles and alignments – the difficulties of interpreting multi-period and incomplete monuments and the nature of some of the observations has rendered Thom's theories an imperfect base for constructing a view of society in Wessex in 2000 BC.

Nevertheless, periods of monument building may be related to periods when power is exercised through ritual and ceremonial, and theocracies can form an intermediate stage in the evolution of ranked societies where power is validated directly through reference to the supernatural. Such societies may build elaborate monuments to those supernatural powers and the building of such massive structures also has political implications. This is a far cry from the temple/residences of astronomer priests and the evidence requires a more moderate view of a stratified society engaging in large-scale public works in 2000 BC as expressions of tribal identity and as focal centres for tribal territories in Wessex. Avebury, Marden, Durrington Walls, Knowlton and Mount Pleasant each have an associated cluster of long and round barrows showing that the heartland of such tribal territory was already being established soon after 3000 BC and that the late Neolithic development was the summation of a process that had been underway for nearly a millennium.

Once built, the monuments – whether dwellings or temples – had a massive physical presence which must have invested them with an important role in legitimating power structures, enhancing ceremonial activities and protecting traditional values from challenge by coming to epitomize past achievements. They were, in effect, a source and a prop of legitimate authority and remained so for some three centuries when, as at Mount Pleasant and Avebury, they were replaced by monuments in stone. By 1000 BC most had been abandoned, showing a break with the past that must have resulted from a change in the ways in which power was exercised and displayed.

Select Bibliography

ATKINSON, R.J.C., 1979 *Stonehenge*, Harmondsworth.

ATKINSON, R.J.C. PIGGOTT, C.M. and SANDARS, N.K. 1951 *Excavations at Dorchester, Oxon. First Report*, Oxford.

BARTRAM, W. 1971 *Travels through North and South Carolina, Georgia, East and West Florida, the Cherokee country, the extensive territories of the Muscogulges or Creek Confederacy and the country of the Choctaws*, University of Georgia.

BRADLEY, R. 1984 *The Social Foundations of Prehistoric Britain*, London.

BURGESS, C. 1980 *The Age of Stonehenge*, London.

BURL, A. 1976 *The Stone Circles of the British Isles*, London and New Haven.

BURL, A. 1979 *Prehistoric Avebury*, London and New Haven.

BURL, A. 1987 *The Stonehenge People*, London.

CALDWELL, J. AND MCCANN, C. 1941 *Irene Mound Site, Chatham County, Georgia*, University of Georgia.

CASTLEDEN, R. 1987 *The Stonehenge People*, London

CHIPPINDALE, C. 1983 *Stonehenge Complete*, London and New York.

CLARK, J.G.D. 1936 The timber monument at Arminghall and its affinities. *Proc. Prehist. Soc.* 2, 1–51.

CLARKE, D.V. 1976 *The Neolithic Village at Skara Brae, Orkney. 1972–73 Excavations*. HMSO, London.

CLARKE, D.V. COWIE, T.G. and FOXON, A. 1985 *Symbols of Power at the time of Stonehenge*. National Museum of Antiquaries of Scotland, Edinburgh.

CLUTTON-BROCK, J. 1984 *Neolithic antler picks from Grimes Graves, Norfolk and Durrington Walls, Wiltshire*. British Museum, London.

CUNNINGTON, M.E. 1929 *Woodhenge*, Devizes.

CUNNINGTON, M.E. 1931 The 'Sanctuary' at Overton Hill, near Avebury. *Wilts. Archaeol. Nat. Hist. Soc.*, 45, 300–335.

DARVILL, T. 1987 *Prehistoric Britain*, London.

EVANS, J.G. 1972 *Landsnails in Archaeology*, London and New York.

FRASER, D. 1983 *Land and Society in Neolithic Orkney*. British Archaeological Reports, Oxford.

MACKIE, E.W. 1977 *Science and Society in Prehistoric Britain*, London and New York.

MERCER, R.J. 1981 The excavation of a late-neolithic henge-type enclosure at Balfarg, Markinch, Fife, Scotland 1977–78. *Proc. Soc. Ants, Scotland*, 111, 63–171.

PIGGOTT, S. and PIGGOTT, C.M. 1939 Stone and earth circles in Dorset. *Antiquity*, 13, 138–158.

PIGGOTT, S. 1940 Timber circles: a re-examination. *Archaeol. Journal*, 96, 193–222.

PRYOR, F. 1978 *Excavation at Fengate, Peterborough, England: the second report.*

RENFREW, C. 1973 *Before Civilization*, London and New York.

ROYAL COMMISSION ON HISTORICAL MONUMENTS (ENGLAND) 1979 *Stonehenge and its Environs*, London.

RICHARDS, C. and THOMAS, J. 1984 Ritual activity and structured deposition in later Neolithic Wessex in R. Bradley and J. Gardiner (eds.) *BAR* 133, 189–218, Oxford.

SMITH, R.W. 1985 *Prehistoric human ecology in the Wessex chalklands*. PhD Thesis. University of Southampton.

STARTIN, B. and BRADLEY, R. 1981 Some notes on work organisation and society in Prehistoric Wessex. In *Astronomy and Society in Britain during the period 4000 – 1500 BC.* British Archaeological Reports, 88, 289–296, Oxford.

THOM, A. 1967 *Megalithic Sites in Britain,* Oxford.

THOM, A 1971 *Megalithic Lunar Observatories,* Oxford.

WAINWRIGHT, G.J. and LONGWORTH, I.H. 1971 *Durrington Walls: Excavations 1966–68.* Rep. Res. Comm. Soc. Antiquaries London 29.

WAINWRIGHT, G.J. 1971 The excavation of a later Neolithic Enclosure at Marden, Wiltshire. *Antiquaries Journal,* 51, 177–239.

WAINWRIGHT, G.J. 1975 Religion and settlement in Wessex 3000–1700 BC in Fowler P.J. (ed.) *Recent work in Rural Archaeology.* Bradford on Avon.

WAINWRIGHT, G.J. 1979 *Mount Pleasant, Dorset: Excavations 1970–1971.* Research Comm. Soc. Antiquaries of London 37.

List of Illustrations

Figures

All figures were redrawn by ML Design.

Index

Figure numbers appear in **bold** and plate numbers in *italic*

SSH
BOOK FOR LOAN